The Quebec Secession Reference

The Rule of Law and the Position of the Attorney General of Canada

WARREN J. NEWMAN

B.A., B.C.L., LL.B.
GENERAL COUNSEL
CONSTITUTIONAL AFFAIRS AND CANADIAN UNITY
DEPARTMENT OF JUSTICE OF CANADA

Published also in French under the title *Le Renvoi relatif à la sécession du Québec : La primauté du droit et la position du procureur général du Canada*.

Printed in Canada.

Canadian Cataloguing in Publication Data

Newman, Warren J.
    The Quebec Secession Reference : the rule of law and the position of the Attorney General of Canada

ISBN 1-55014-384-0

1. Secession—Quebec (Province).   2. Constitutional law—Canada.
3. Quebec (Province)—History—Autonomy and independence movements.
4. Self-determination, National—Quebec (Province).   5. Canada. Dept.
of Justice.   I. York University (Toronto, Ont.). Centre for Public Law
and Public Policy.   II. Title.

KE4216.35.S42N48 1999   3542.71′039   C99-932476-4
KF4483.A4N48 1999

To my wife Julie and our daughters Véronique and Émilie

Contents

Preface

This book began as a conference paper for the 1998 Constitutional Cases Symposium held on April 16, 1999 under the auspices of the Professional Development Programme of Osgoode Hall Law School at York University, Toronto. The Symposium was co-chaired by Daniel Drache, Director of the Robarts Centre for Canadian Studies and Professor of Political Science at York University, and by Patrick J. Monahan, Director of the York University Centre for Public Law and Public Policy and Professor of Law at Osgoode Hall Law School. The Symposium was billed as "An Analysis of the 1998 Constitutional Decisions of the Supreme Court of Canada." I was asked, as one who had appeared as co-counsel for the Attorney General of Canada in the *Quebec Secession Reference*, to present my observations on the implications of the Reference.

What follows is an analytical memoir, crafted from the perspective of a constitutional lawyer acting on behalf of the federal government, on the political and legal events that led to the making of the Reference, on the arguments put forward in support of the federal position, and on the outcome and the wisdom of the Reference opinion rendered by the Supreme Court. To the extent that this book summarizes the position of the Attorney General of Canada in the *Bertrand* case and the Reference proceedings, it is an accurate reflection of that position. To the extent that the book offers personal views and insights, those views are my own (although I would hope that they are shared by many), and they should not, of course, be taken as binding upon the Department of Justice or the Government of Canada.

The text was written as a piece in February and March 1999 and benefited from the wise and helpful comments of Mary Dawson, Q.C., Associate Deputy Minister of the Department of Justice and responsible for Constitutional Affairs and Canadian Unity. The preparation of the French-language version offered me another occasion to correct minor typographical errors and infelicities that had escaped first reading. Having reviewed the manuscript again for publication, I have decided not to revise its substantive contents, save for updating a footnote or two that refer to cases currently before the courts.

My resistance to any temptation I might have had to embellish the text with additional commentary at this point stems first from a desire to preserve the immediacy, timeliness, and focus of the piece, which was conceived and written in the aftermath of the Reference and which should be approached by the reader as such. It also stems from an appropriate sense of professional responsibility as a practitioner in the field of constitutional law. Since the writing of the original conference paper, I have had to argue the meaning of the Supreme Court's opinion in the *Quebec Secession Reference* before appellate courts in two provinces. It is evident that from a legal standpoint the Reference opinion will continue to be invoked in proceedings before the courts, and that the courts will have to determine its relevance with respect to a number of looming constitutional issues. To take but one example, to what degree, if any, does the *Quebec Secession Reference* affect the distinction between constitutional *principles* and constitutional *provisions*? Constitutional judicial review in Canada has been heretofore largely founded upon the rule, expressed in the words of s. 52(1) of the *Constitution Act, 1982*, that any law that is inconsistent with the *provisions* of the Constitution is invalid and of no force and effect. Has the Supreme Court's emphasis on constitutional principles (albeit in the specific context of the secession of a province, and while affirming the primacy of the written Constitution) made more plausible claims that the courts should have a role in reviewing and perhaps even striking down laws allegedly enacted in contravention of broad and open-ended constitutional principles, even where the provisions of the Constitution are arguably not engaged in the debate over the validity of the impugned legislation? As fascinating— to political scientists and constitutional lawyers, at least—as this issue and several others arising from the *Quebec Secession Reference* may be, I will naturally forbear from pronouncing upon them in the context of this book. They must be left to another day, and to another forum.

Beyond the immediate concerns of constitutional litigation, there is also the greater issue of the future of the country and the continuing debate over Quebec's place within the Canadian federation. The current Government of Quebec remains committed to establishing "winning conditions" for a third Quebec sovereignty referendum. I have already said all that prudence would dictate on this volatile matter in the body of the text, particularly in Chapter 4, dealing with the aftermath of the Reference and the lessons to be learned from the Supreme Court's immensely instructive reasoning.

At the outset of the text I have acknowledged the outstanding contribution of my colleagues and fellow counsel to the development of the position of the Attorney General of Canada in the *Quebec Secession Reference*. This was truly the fruit of the collective efforts of an exemplary team, under the leadership of Mary Dawson, the inspiration of our lead counsel, Yves Fortier, and the guidance of the Privy Council Office and our respective Ministers. It was a privilege to have been a part of that team.

Finally, I would like especially to thank Professor Patrick Monahan, who generously extended the invitation to me to speak at the Constitutional Cases Symposium, and who encouraged and ultimately ensured the publication of this volume.

W.J.N.
August 1999

About the Author

Warren Newman is General Counsel, Constitutional Affairs and Canadian Unity, for the Department of Justice of Canada. He was co-counsel for the Attorney General of Canada before the Supreme Court of Canada in the *Quebec Secession Reference* and in the *Bertrand* case before the Superior Court of Quebec. He has also appeared as co-counsel in a number of other significant constitutional cases before the Supreme Court of Canada, including the *Manitoba Language Rights Reference*, the *Bilodeau* case, the *Brunet* case, and the *Reference re Manitoba Public Schools Act*, as well as before trial and appellate courts in other constitutional litigation.

Mr. Newman graduated with a D.C.S. in arts, a B.A. in history and political science, a B.C.L. in civil law and an LL.B. in common law from McGill University, where he was a University and a National Program Scholar. He is a member of the Bars of Quebec and Ontario. Mr. Newman has been actively interested and involved in constitutional law issues for more than twenty years.

From 1982 to 1984, Mr. Newman was the legal policy advisor to the Commissioner of Official Languages for Canada. After working as a policy analyst at the Federal-Provincial Relations Office, Mr. Newman was seconded to the Human Rights Law Section of the Department of Justice in 1985 to develop the legislative proposals that led to the enactment of Bill C-72, the 1988 *Official Languages Act*, and he acted as the instructing officer on the drafting of the legislation. In 1990, Mr. Newman was appointed Senior Counsel and the first Director of the Official Languages Law Group. In 1994 he was named Special Advisor to the Associate Deputy Minister, Public Law, with responsibility for coordinating constitutional law and policy advice on national unity issues, before forming part of the Canadian Unity Group in 1996 as Senior Counsel and Litigation Coordinator. He was appointed General Counsel and Senior Coordinator of the Group in 1997.

Mr. Newman has testified as an expert witness before several Parliamentary Committees dealing with constitutional affairs. He has spoken at a number of academic conferences and several of his papers have been published. In 1989 Mr. Newman received the Deputy Minister of Justice's Prize for Professional Excellence for his work in the field of language rights; in 1997, a Merit Award from the Deputy Minister for his contribution to the drafting of the Attorney General of Canada's submissions in the *Quebec Secession Reference*; and in 1998, an Award of Distinction from the Minister of Justice for his commitment to Canada's linguistic and legal duality.

1

Introduction

Le présent renvoi allie des questions juridiques et constitutionnelles des plus subtiles et complexes à des questions politiques très délicates.

This Reference combines legal and constitutional questions of the utmost subtlety and complexity with political questions of great sensitivity.

With these words, counsel for the Attorney General of Canada began oral argument on February 16, 1998, in the *Quebec Secession Reference*.[1] The words are, of course, the opening ones of the Supreme Court of Canada's opinion in the *Manitoba Language Rights Reference*,[2] a judgment that has stood for over a decade as a powerful testimonial to the Court's commitment to its duty to ensure respect for the integrity of the Constitution and to protect the rule of law, even in the face of long-standing, sweeping illegality sanctioned by the legislature.

In the *Quebec Secession Reference*, the Supreme Court once again rose to the occasion. In a constitutional case that generally has been described, with more understatement than hyperbole, as one of the most important the Court has ever had to consider, the nine judges of the Court resolved to come together as one and to render a remarkably compelling ruling on some of the most basic legal issues relating to the secession of Quebec from Canada. The Court did so despite a heightened political climate surrounding the Reference that made the Court's role—already difficult—especially sensitive, controversial, and subject to scrutiny. And the Court's wisdom in its treatment of these issues found broad adherence in both federalist and sovereigntist circles alike; no mean feat when one considers how polarized these two camps had been with regard to the legitimacy of the Reference as a means of seeking clarification from the courts on the legality of the secession process. Canadians and particularly Quebecers can take pride in the Supreme Court's masterful handling of the issues in the *Quebec Secession Reference*.

---

[1] *Reference re Secession of Quebec*, [1998] 2 S.C.R. 217; 161 D.L.R. (4th) 385; 228 N.R. 203. The citations in this book are to the paragraph numbers of the Reference judgment, which are common to all of the law reports.

[2] *Reference re Manitoba Language Rights*, [1985] S.C.R. 721, at p. 728. The Court also found those words to be apposite in commencing its opinion in the *Quebec Secession Reference*: "This Reference requires us to consider momentous questions that go to the heart of our system of constitutional government. The observation we made more than a decade ago in *Reference re Manitoba Language Rights* [...] applies with equal force here": *Reference re Secession of Quebec, supra*, para. 1.

This book is written from the viewpoint of a constitutional lawyer with the Department of Justice who acted as one of counsel[3] to the Attorney General of Canada in the *Quebec Secession Reference*. While the book is the work of an individual, it is also, in passages outlining the federal position in the Reference, a synthesis of the materials developed by the collective efforts of a dedicated team,[4] and it naturally carries with it some of the advocacy that the role of counsel to the Attorney General of Canada required in the Reference. It does not pretend to be an exhaustive account of the complex series of actions, statements, and events leading up to the Reference, nor of all the arguments that were advanced in the Reference by the *amicus curiae*, the Attorneys General of the provinces and the Ministers of Justice of the territories, as well as the other interveners; arguments that immeasurably enriched the legal debate. It would require a treatise, drawing on the disciplines not only of law, but also of history and political science, to appreciate fully the significance of the *Quebec Secession Reference* and to place it in its larger societal context.

My goals have been more modest. In Chapter 2, I have attempted only to highlight the most salient legal and political events that led to the actual making of the Reference, and to outline the position that the Government of Canada, as represented by the Attorney General of Canada, developed and put forward to deal with the legal issues arising from the Government of Quebec's Draft *Act respecting the sovereignty of Québec* and its successor, Bill 1. The premises of the draft sovereignty legislation, insofar as it purported to authorize the National Assembly of Quebec to effect the *unilateral* secession of Quebec from Canada, represented an unprecedented, albeit still inchoate, challenge to the Canadian legal order and the values upon which that order is predicated. Not the least of those values is respect for the rule of law and the role of the Constitution and the courts in controlling the exercise of governmental power and in permitting political decisions to be made within an orderly, stable framework of fundamental legal rules.

---

[3] Counsel appearing before the Supreme Court of Canada on behalf of the Attorney General of Canada in the Reference were L. Yves Fortier, C.C., Q.C., Chairman and senior partner of the law firm of Ogilvy Renault, Canada's former Ambassador to the United Nations, and now President of the London Court of International Arbitration; Pierre Bienvenu, also a partner with Ogilvy Renault, and co-counsel in the *Bertrand* case; Warren J. Newman, General Counsel and Litigation Coordinator, Canadian Unity Group; Jean-Marc Aubry, Q.C., Senior General Counsel, Civil Litigation Section; and Mary E. Dawson, Q.C., Associate Deputy Minister, Department of Justice of Canada.

[4] The preparation and drafting of the Attorney General of Canada's position were carried out under the leadership of Mary Dawson by counsel and by the lawyers of the Canadian Unity Group of the Department of Justice, which included, at various times throughout the Reference proceedings, Michael Delaney, Warren Newman, Jason Reiskind, Andrew Saranchuk, Josée Touchette, Marc Tremblay, Alan Willis, Laurie Wright, and Stephen Zaluski. The author of this book would also like to acknowledge the important contribution of other specialists in constitutional law and international law, both within and outside the Department; of the experts retained by counsel, particularly Professor James Crawford of Cambridge University; and of the senior officials and officers of the Intergovernmental Affairs sector of the Privy Council Office, most notably George Anderson, Graham Flack, and John McDowell.

In Chapter 3, dealing with the Reference proceedings themselves, I have tried to provide a faithful analysis of the Supreme Court of Canada's opinion on the issues raised by the Reference questions, and to highlight some of the links between the Court's opinion and the position of the Attorney General of Canada. The Court's opinion, which, as in all reference cases, is presented in the form of a judgment, is one of the most well-written decisions that the Court has rendered. It is a delicately balanced, incisive, and highly persuasive piece of legal reasoning that clarifies many difficult issues and that combines clear exposition with subtle and sophisticated messaging. The judgment of the Court must be read as a whole, and it would be to the detriment of one's overall understanding and appreciation to isolate one particular paragraph or pronouncement out of context, and thereby to miss its relationship to the rest. For the first time in memory, the Court chose not to issue a formal order answering the Reference questions as such. The answers to the questions are to be found in the intricately woven responses that comprise the reasons for judgment of the Court.

Finally, in Chapter 4, I have tried to provide some flavour of the early reaction to the judgment, and to suggest some of the lessons that we, as jurists and Canadians, can draw from the Court's wisdom and sage guidance as we approach the events and challenges facing the future of the country in the years to come.

2

The Key Events Leading to the Reference

The Draft Bill, *An Act respecting the sovereignty of Québec*

What key events preceded the Reference by the Governor in Council to the Supreme Court of Canada, for hearing and consideration, of a series of questions on whether the National Assembly, legislature, or government of Quebec had the power under the Constitution of Canada, or a right at international law, to effect the secession of Quebec from Canada unilaterally? That story began in the National Assembly on December 6, 1994 with the tabling, by the Premier of Quebec, of a Draft Bill entitled *An Act respecting the sovereignty of Québec*. The explanatory notes accompanying the Bill defined Quebec's sovereignty as being

> the accession of Québec to a position of exclusive jurisdiction, through its democratic institutions, to make laws and levy taxes in its territory and to act on the international scene for the making of agreements and treaties of any kind with other independent States and to participate in various international organizations.

Under the heading, "The Process," the notes set out six steps for Quebec's "accession to sovereignty":

> 1. publication of the draft bill;
>
> 2. a period of information and participation for the purposes of improving the bill and drafting the "Declaration of sovereignty" which will form the preamble to the bill;
>
> 3. discussion of the bill respecting the sovereignty of Québec, and passage by the National Assembly;
>
> 4. approval of the Act by the population in a referendum;
>
> 5. a period of discussions with Canada on the transitional measures to be set in place, particularly as regards the apportionment of property and debts; during this period the new Québec constitution will be drafted;
>
> 6. the accession of Québec to sovereignty.

Nowhere could the process, as set out in the explanatory notes and the Premier of Quebec's statements accompanying the tabling of the Draft Bill, be said to contemplate, expressly or implicitly, an amendment to the Constitution of Canada to effect the secession of the province. The "Declaration of sovereignty" that the Premier had in mind would be drafted "un peu sur le modèle de la Déclaration d'indépendance américaine";[1] in other words, it could amount to a unilateral declaration of independence (a U.D.I.). As Mr. Parizeau later admitted, with revealing but disturbing candour, in his book, *Pour un Québec souverain*,

> On constatera que mes discours, en ce qui touche les négociations avec le Canada, sont rédigés de façon à permettre une telle déclaration de souveraineté. Et je ne me suis jamais engagé en public ou en privé à ne pas faire de déclaration unilatérale de souveraineté. Tout ce qui a été écrit dans les journaux à ce sujet démontre une fois de plus que, dans ces matières, ceux qui parlent ne savent pas et que ceux qui savent ne parlent pas.[2]

It was immediately evident that what was set out in the Draft Bill was patently unconstitutional and *ultra vires* the legislature of Quebec—in point of law, a radical nullity. The Draft Bill, if enacted, would have purported to declare that "Quebec is a sovereign country." The Government of Quebec would be authorized to conclude an agreement on economic association with the Government of Canada. A new constitution for Quebec would be enacted "in accordance with the procedure determined by the National Assembly" (s. 3). Quebec would retain its current boundaries (s. 4). Quebec citizenship would be established (s. 5). The Canadian dollar would be retained as the legal currency of Quebec (s. 6). Canada's rights and obligations under international treaties and conventions would be assumed by Quebec (s. 7). The Government of Quebec would be authorized to apply for admission to the United Nations and other international organizations. Quebec's membership in the Commonwealth, la Francophonie, NATO, NORAD, NAFTA, and the GATT were also dealt with.

The Draft Bill also provided (in s. 10) that "Laws passed by the Parliament of Canada [...] shall remain in force until amended or repealed by the National Assembly." Pensions, supplements, permits, licences, and authorizations would be continued (s. 11). The courts of civil and criminal jurisdiction would be continued as well (s. 12), and the Quebec Court of Appeal "shall become the court of highest jurisdiction until a Supreme Court is established" under the new constitution. The continuity of various appointments, as well as of the laws, rules, and conventions governing the internal constitution of Quebec and access to English-language schools, would also be maintained until the new constitution came into force (ss. 13, 14). The Government of Quebec would be authorized to conclude an agreement with Canada relating to property and debt apportionment and other matters (s. 15).

Section 16 of the Draft Bill declared that "This Act comes into force one year after its approval by referendum, unless the National Assembly fixes an earlier date." Sections 2, 3, and 15, however, were to "come into force

---

[1] Government of Quebec, *La Participation des citoyens au projet de la souveraineté*, document tabled in the National Assembly by Premier Jacques Parizeau with the Draft Sovereignty Bill (6 December 1994).

[2] Jacques Parizeau, *Pour un Québec souverain* (Montreal: vlb éditeur), p. 286. The book was published by the former Premier in May 1997, and caused great consternation in sovereigntist circles.

on the day following the day this Act is approved by referendum." Approval by a majority of votes cast in a referendum would be required for the legislation to come into force[3] (s. 17), and the referendum question would be as follows:

> Are you in favour of the Act passed by the National Assembly declaring the sovereignty of Québec? YES or NO

This brief overview of the provisions of the Draft *Act respecting the sovereignty of Québec* provides an indication of how sweeping in scope was the proposed legislation. What it portended was nothing less than a revolution, an overthrow of the established legal order of Canada. But it was a revolution that dared not speak its name. The "Declaration of sovereignty" was to be clothed in statutory form, and on its face the Act would promise continuity, not chaos. However, by an artful sleight of hand, the legislature of the province of Quebec, which exercises its powers under the Constitution of Canada, would be replaced by the National Assembly of the independent state of Quebec, exercising powers under the new régime purportedly established by the sovereignty legislation itself.[4]

So why was the proposed sovereignty legislation not challenged immediately in litigation before the courts if it was *ultra vires* the legislature? The answer lies primarily in the fact that the *Act respecting the sovereignty of Québec* was, at this early stage, only a draft bill, roughly equivalent to a white paper. Certainly, the prevailing view was that any attempt to litigate its validity at that time would likely be ruled by the courts to be premature and, quite possibly, an unwarranted interference in the legislative process.[5]

---

[3] The steps comprising the actual enactment of the proposed *Act respecting the sovereignty of Québec* must be distinguished from the provisions of the Draft Bill respecting its coming into force. These steps are further obscured by the fact that the Quebec *Referendum Act*, R.S.Q., c. C-64.1, contains, notably in s. 10, certain rules relating to the manner and form by which bills made subject to consultation by referendum may be enacted. Section 10 provides: "A bill adopted by the National Assembly cannot be submitted to a referendum unless it contains, at the time of being tabled, a provision to that effect, as well as the text of the question submitted for referendum. This bill cannot be presented for assent until it has been submitted to the electors by way of a referendum." The *Act respecting the sovereignty of Québec*, the "Act passed by the National Assembly of Québec" contemplated in the referendum question set out in the Draft Bill, could not in any event have become law under our legal system unless and until assented to by the Lieutenant Governor, who is an integral part of the legislature of Quebec (s. 71, *Constitution Act, 1867*; s. 41, *Constitution Act, 1982*). The National Assembly, despite common parlance, is only *part* of the legislature; the legislative assembly of a province cannot enact legislation on its own. The referendum question in the Draft Bill tended to convey the impression that the "Act" would already have been, at the time of the referendum, a law of Quebec and not simply a bill passed but not yet assented to. This would seem to cloak the proposed legislation in the mantle of apparent legitimacy attending a duly enacted statute of the legislature, while shielding the "Act" from the scrutiny of the courts because it was in truth still only a bill.

[4] This bootstrap exercise of transferring powers to the National Assembly would later be accentuated in Bill 1, *An Act respecting the future of Québec*, the successor to the Draft Bill, discussed *infra*.

[5] In *Reference re Resolution to amend the Constitution*, [1981] 1 S.C.R. 753 at p. 785, the majority of the Supreme Court stated: "Courts come into the picture when legislation is

Early Requests for a Reference

It should come as no surprise, then, that a request was made by a group of concerned citizens, within days of the tabling of the Draft Bill, for a reference on the validity of the proposed legislation.[6] The Prime Minister replied that although he understood why the group would want to see the legality of the Draft Bill questioned, "I do not agree that, in the present circumstances, the course you are recommending would be an advisable one for the Government of Canada." The Prime Minister stated that "the central issue in the months ahead is whether or not the citizens of Quebec want to stay in Canada, and that we should not allow ourselves to be side-tracked into a discussion of how separation might occur." The best way of dealing with the issue at that time was to make sure that those who advocated secession "carry the burden of proof to show why separating from Canada would be in the best interests of Quebecers."

This determination to focus on the concrete *why* of separation (i.e., secession), rather than being drawn into an early and deep examination of the legal mechanics of *how* it might take place, was a centrepoint of federal government policy in the months preceding the referendum campaign. A so-called "legalistic" approach at this stage could well have been perceived as heavy-handed, and worse, been portrayed as an attempt to intimidate or to prevent the population of Quebec from expressing its views democratically. This would have been counter-productive. A hearing before the Supreme

---

enacted and not before (unless references are made to them for their opinion on a bill or a proposed enactment)." In *Reference re Canada Assistance Plan (B.C.)*, [1991] 2 S.C.R. 525, at p. 559, Sopinka J., writing for the Court, observed: "The formulation and introduction of a bill are part of the legislative process with which the courts will not meddle." For a more recent example of this view, see the reasons for judgment of Williamson J. of the Supreme Court of British Columbia rendered on February 5, 1999 in *Gordon Campbell et al. v. A.G. B.C., A.G. Canada and the Nisga'a Tribal Council* (Vancouver, docket A982738) in which the Court adjourned the setting of a date for the hearing of the challenge brought by the plaintiffs to the ratification of the final agreement among Canada, British Columbia, and the Nisga'a Nation until after the enactment of settlement legislation by the legislature of the province and by Parliament. "Under our system of government, it is essential that the courts respect the right of Parliament and of the legislative assemblies to exercise unfettered freedom in the formulation, tabling, amendment, and passage of legislation. [...] The legislative branch must be given free reign to introduce bills and to explore in debate the ramifications of proposed legislation. Legislatures are, nonetheless, bound by the rule of law. Should they pass legislation which the courts find to be unconstitutional, they are bound to respect such a ruling." (Paras. 28 and 29.)

[6] On December 9, 1994, three days after the tabling of the Draft Bill, counsel for the Special Committee on Canadian Unity, a group of concerned citizens in Quebec, wrote to the Prime Minister of Canada to request that the Governor in Council immediately refer the following question to the Supreme Court of Canada: "Is it within the legislative authority of a province of Canada, under the Constitution of Canada, to enact a statute declaring that province to be a sovereign state; and if such a statute is enacted, what is its force or effect?" (The letter and the Prime Minister's response thereto were filed of record by the Attorney General of Canada in the materials forming the "Case on Appeal" in the *Quebec Secession Reference*; see Case, vol. 1, tabs 7 and 8, pp. 79 to 83.) Members of the Special Committee on Canadian Unity later commenced a challenge to the validity of the Draft Bill's successor, Bill 1; see *Singh et al. v. Attorney General of Quebec*, discussed *infra*.

Court of Canada on the eve of the referendum would likely have divided federalist forces, aroused passions, and shed more heat than light.

Beyond these policy considerations, it must be remembered that informal requests for references to the Supreme Court of Canada are conveyed to the federal government with frequent regularity. Some would believe that, in an ideal world, the Government of Canada should refer every important or topical legal issue to the Court for its opinion. However, the reference function is, as the *Supreme Court Act* states, a "special jurisdiction".[7] The Court's primary role is that of a "General Court of Appeal for Canada".[8] While the Court's advisory jurisdiction is not incompatible with its adjudicative and appellate function, and while the opinions rendered by the Court under the reference procedure have made a profound contribution to Canadian constitutional and public law, it is a procedure that must be used parsimoniously and with appropriate circumspection by the Governor in Council.

The "Tripartite Agreement"

On June 12, 1995, the leaders of the Parti Québécois (Premier Parizeau), the Bloc Québécois (Lucien Bouchard), and the Action Démocratique du Québec (Mario Dumont) concluded a "tripartite agreement" by which, following a YES majority vote in the referendum,

> the National Assembly, on the one hand, will be empowered to proclaim the sovereignty of Québec, and the government, on the other hand, will be bound to propose to Canada a treaty on a new economic and political Partnership, so as to, among other things, consolidate the existing economic space.

The process for "accession to sovereignty" was described in the agreement as follows:

> Insofar as the negotiations unfold in a positive fashion, the National Assembly will declare the sovereignty of Québec after an agreement is reached on the Partnership treaty. One of the first acts of a sovereign Québec will be ratification of a Partnership treaty.
>
> The negotiations will not exceed one year, unless the National Assembly decides otherwise.
>
> If the negotiations prove to be fruitless, the National Assembly will be empowered to declare the sovereignty of Québec without further delay.

The conclusion of this agreement among the leaders of the Quebec political parties supporting the sovereigntist option in the referendum marked the beginning of the "virage," the "question gagnante," and the "conditions gagnantes" that Mr. Bouchard had been pressing for in order to move the sovereigntists ahead in the polls. A very marked and rapid upswing in sovereigntist support later took place when Mr. Bouchard was appointed "négociateur en chef" by Mr. Parizeau and now led the campaign on a

---

[7] *Supreme Court Act*, R.S.C. 1985, c. S-26, s. 53 (title).

[8] *Constitution Act, 1867*, s. 101.

sovereignty-partnership theme, placing the emphasis on continuing economic and political partnership with Canada. The "tripartite agreement" would be incorporated and scheduled to Bill 1, the Draft Bill's successor. However, the "negotiations" contemplated were on the drafting of a treaty between sovereign states, nowhere on an amendment to the Constitution of Canada to effect the secession itself. Furthermore, if negotiations on a treaty failed, the National Assembly would still be able to declare Quebec's independence unilaterally. That a U.D.I. was still in the cards was confirmed, once again, by former Premier Parizeau:

> Je ne comprends pas ceux que les mots effraient. Une déclaration unilatérale de souveraineté du Québec faisait partie intégrante de la loi et de l'Entente du 12 juin, advenant un échec des négociations de partenariat.[9]

The *Bertrand* Case

On July 31, 1995, a lawyer in Quebec City, Mr. Guy Bertrand, wrote to the Attorney General of Quebec requesting a reference to the Court of Appeal of the province on the validity of the Draft Bill and unilateral secession. No response was forthcoming. Mr. Bertrand sent similar letters to the Prime Minister and the Attorney General of Canada.[10] On August 10, 1995, Mr. Bertrand filed an action for declaratory judgment and permanent injunction in the Superior Court of Quebec challenging the constitutional validity of the Draft Bill and the Government of Quebec's process for "accession to sovereignty." Mr. Bertrand also filed a motion for interlocutory measures, seeking declaratory and injunctive relief against the legality and the holding of the upcoming sovereignty referendum itself, to the extent it was directed to illegal and unconstitutional ends. The Attorney General of Canada, who had been impleaded as a third-party mis en cause, chose not to appear in the proceedings.

On August 24, 1995, the Attorney General of Quebec filed a motion to dismiss Mr. Bertrand's motion for interlocutory relief directed against the legality and the holding of the sovereignty referendum, arguing that the petitioner was seeking to have the Court interfere in the legislative powers, functions, and privileges of the National Assembly, and that the referendum

---

[9] "Déclaration de monsieur Jacques Parizeau" (news release), May 8, 1997, filed of record in the Supreme Court by the Attorney General of Canada in the *Quebec Secession Reference*; Case, addendum II, tab 3, at p. 13.

[10] In their replies (of August 14 and August 9, 1995, respectively), the Prime Minister and the Attorney General of Canada provided substantially the same response that was given several months earlier to the Special Committee on Canadian Unity. The Honourable Allan Rock wrote: "Je saisis bien les préoccupations juridiques que vous soulevez, mais nous croyons cependant qu'à l'heure actuelle la véritable question n'est pas comment la séparation pourrait éventuellement se faire, mais est-ce que les Québécois veulent toujours faire partie du Canada. C'est au gouvernement du Québec de faire la démonstration que la séparation serait dans les meilleurs intérêts des Québécois. Nous croyons fermement que si on pose la question clairement et sans équivoque aux Québécois, ils choisiraient toujours de rester partie intégrante de notre pays." This correspondence was filed of record by the Attorney General of Canada in the *Quebec Secession Reference*; Case, vol. II, tabs 12 to 15, pp. 339–354.

and the referendum process were part of a "démarche démocratique fondamentale qui trouve sa sanction dans le droit international public et dont l'opportunité n'a pas à être debattue devant les tribunaux."[11] The Attorney General of Quebec added in his motion that

> La tenue du référendum en cause a pour fondement le principe démocratique et il s'agit d'une question qui ne relève pas de la juris-diction des tribunaux.

On August 31, 1995, Mr. Justice Robert Lesage of the Superior Court of Quebec denied the Attorney General of Quebec's motion to dismiss and decided to hear Mr. Bertrand's motion for an interlocutory injunction and declaratory judgment. Mr. Justice Lesage wrote:

> La menace que le Gouvernement du Québec ferait porter aux institutions politiques de la fédération canadienne est une question grave et sérieuse, qui de sa nature est justiciable en regard de la Constitution du Canada.[12]

At that point, counsel for the Attorney General of Quebec withdrew from further participation in the hearing on the motion. On September 5, 1995, the Premier of Quebec wrote[13] to the Speaker of the National Assembly to request that he convene an emergency sitting of the Assembly for the pur-pose of introducing a bill on the future of Quebec, as well as a referendum question in accordance with ss. 8 and 9 of the *Referendum Act*. He added:

> L'Assemblée pourra également être saisie, si besoin est, de toute mesure propre à affirmer ses droits, privilèges et prérogatives, à protéger ses travaux contre toute ingérence et à garantir que le peuple du Québec pourra effectivement se prononcer sur son avenir.

Bill 1, *An Act respecting the future of Québec*

On September 7, 1995, at the extraordinary sitting of the Assembly, the Premier introduced Bill 1, *An Act respecting the future of Québec*. The "Declaration of sovereignty" that now formed the preamble to the Bill stated, in its final recital:

> We, the people of Québec, through our National Assembly, proclaim:

> Québec is a sovereign country.

Sections 1 and 2 of Bill 1 provided, under the respective rubrics "SELF-DETERMINATION" and "SOVEREIGNTY," as follows:

> 1. The National Assembly is authorized, within the scope of this act, to proclaim the sovereignty of Québec.

> The proclamation must be preceded by a formal offer of economic and political partnership with Canada.

---

[11] Motion of Attorney General of Quebec to dismiss Mr. Bertrand's motion for interlocutory measures, *Bertrand v. Bégin et al.* (24 August 1995), Sup. Ct. of Quebec 200-05-002117-955.

[12] Interlocutory order of Lesage J. in *Bertrand v. Bégin, supra* (31 August 1995).

[13] Letter of Premier Parizeau to Speaker Roger Bertrand, National Assembly (5 September 1995); tabled by the Speaker on September 7, 1995.

2. On the date fixed in the proclamation of the National Assembly, the Declaration of sovereignty appearing in the Preamble shall take effect and Québec shall become a sovereign country; it shall acquire the exclusive power to pass all its laws, levy all its taxes and conclude all its treaties.

Section 3 of Bill 1 bound the Government of Quebec to propose to Canada "a treaty of economic and political partnership based on the tripartite agreement" signed by sovereigntist leaders on June 12, 1995, and now reproduced in the schedule to Bill 1. The treaty required the approval of the National Assembly before ratification. Sections 4 and 5 provided for the establishment of a committee appointed by the Government of Quebec to orient and supervise the negotiations on the partnership treaty.

Section 26 of Bill 1 stated:

26. The negotiations relating to the conclusion of the partnership treaty must not extend beyond October 30, 1996, unless the National Assembly decides otherwise.

The proclamation of sovereignty may be made as soon as the partnership treaty has been approved by the National Assembly or as soon as the latter, after requesting the opinion of the orientation and supervision committee, has concluded that the negotiations have proved fruitless.

The other provisions of Bill 1 were similar to those of the Draft Bill, but more detailed. They dealt with the new constitution (ss. 6 through 9), territory (s. 10), citizenship (ss. 11 to 13), currency (s. 14), treaties, international organizations and alliances (ss. 15 to 17), continuity of law, pensions, benefits, licences and permits, contracts and courts of justice (ss. 18 to 22), federal public servants and employees (s. 23), an interim constitution (s. 24), and agreements in addition to the partnership treaty (s. 25).

At the same time that Premier Parizeau introduced Bill 1, he tabled a new referendum question:[14]

Do you agree that Québec should become sovereign, after having made a formal offer to Canada for a new Economic and Political Partnership, within the scope of the Bill respecting the future of Québec and of the agreement signed on June 12, 1995?

The Judgment of Mr. Justice Lesage in the *Bertrand* Case

On September 8, 1995, Mr. Justice Lesage rendered judgment for the Superior Court of Quebec in the *Bertrand* case proceedings on the motion for

---

[14] *Quare* whether the Quebec *Referendum Act* permits a referendum question to refer to a bill when that referendum question is not part of the bill itself. The referendum question accompanying Bill 1 was not contained in the Bill (unlike the previous question proposed in the Draft Bill), nor was the Bill adopted by the National Assembly before the referendum was held. Section 7 of the *Referendum Act* provides that electors may be consulted by referendum "on a question approved by the National Assembly [...] *or* on a bill *adopted by*

interlocutory relief. He refused to grant an injunction to prevent the holding of the referendum, conscious and concerned as he was about the proper role of the courts and the negative effect injunctive relief would have on political expression. Lesage J. stated in this regard:

> The court cannot prevent the political forces from operating. [...] The court cannot, of course, paralyze the functioning of the National Assembly or prohibit it from debating the issue. That would be an infringement of parliamentary privileges. Moreover, it is preferable that the public discussion be held with full knowledge of the facts. [...] I take judicial notice that neither the official opposition in Quebec nor the federal government intends to block the holding of the referendum. It must be understood that the people wish to express themselves. To issue an injunction against the holding of the referendum would risk creating a greater wrong than the wrong that it is sought to prevent.[15]

At the same time, Lesage J. was at least equally concerned about ensuring that the Constitution and the rule of law were not flouted with impunity:

> On the other hand, it [the Court] cannot approve a violation of the constitutional order. The events that have been set in motion by the Government of Quebec may lead to such a violation. This is not pure speculation. The government is going to very great lengths to get its way. Using its political authority and public moneys, it is seeking to overthrow the constitutional order. [...] The threat is a serious one.[16]

While the Court would not interfere with the referendum process itself, it had no difficulty recognizing the threat that the Draft Bill itself represented to the Constitution of Canada and to the rights and freedoms protected thereunder.[17]

> All of the actions taken by the Quebec government, and the procedure described in the draft bill, indicate that the government, through the Prime Minister and other Cabinet ministers, has undertaken, on behalf of Quebec, to proceed with a unilateral declaration of independence and to obtain Quebec's recognition as a state distinct from Canada.
>
> It is manifest, if not expressly stated, that the Quebec government has no intention of resorting to the amending formula in the Constitution

---

the National Assembly in accordance with section 10." (Emphasis added.) Section 10 provides: "A bill adopted by the National Assembly cannot be submitted to a referendum unless it contains, at the time of being tabled, a provision to that effect, as well as the text of the question submitted for the referendum."

[15] *Bertrand c. Bégin*, [1996] R.J.Q. 2393 (September 8, 1995). The citations in this book are from the English translation of the decision in the Dominion Law Reports: *Bertrand v. Quebec (A.G.)*, 127 D.L.R. (4th) 408, at pp. 429 and 431.

[16] *Id.*, at p. 429.

[17] The Court (*ibid.*, at p. 419) accepted the plaintiff's characterization of the Draft Bill as governmental activity subject to scrutiny under the *Canadian Charter of Rights and Freedoms*. "The draft bill respecting sovereignty is not an Act of the National Assembly. It is not a bill tabled on first reading, but a political document of the government. Parliamentary privilege cannot be invoked in its regard, since such privilege adheres not to the government but to the National Assembly."

to accomplish the secession of Quebec. In this regard, the Quebec government is giving itself a mandate that the Constitution of Canada does not confer on it.

The actions taken by the Government of Quebec in view of the secession of Quebec are a repudiation of the Constitution of Canada. [...] The constitutional change proposed by the Government of Quebec would result in a break in continuity in the legal order, which is manifestly contrary to the Constitution of Canada.[18]

In the circumstances, the Court decided to issue a declaratory judgment, noting that "a declaratory judgment may be just as if not more effective than an injunction."

Moreover, it is the remedy favoured by the courts in constitutional matters, for a variety of reasons. The declaration is not an intrusion into the functioning of the executive or the legislature. It does not open the door to execution proceedings that might appear odious. On the contrary, it allows governments to conceive of ways in which to satisfy the judicial declaration, and thus helps to maintain the balance in our democratic institutions.[19]

Mr. Justice Lesage declared that "a bill that reiterates the terms of the agreement ratified and executed on June 12, 1995, by Messrs. Jacques Parizeau, Lucien Bouchard and Mario Dumont, that would grant the National Assembly of Quebec the capacity or power to declare the sovereignty of Quebec without following the amending procedure provided for in the Constitution of Canada, constitutes a serious threat to the rights or freedoms of the plaintiff guaranteed by the *Canadian Charter of Rights and Freedoms*."[20] In the dispositive part of his ruling, Lesage J. adapted that declaration by referring specifically to Bill 1, which had been introduced the day before his judgment. The Court

DECLARES that Bill 1, entitled an *Act respecting the future of Québec*, introduced by Prime Minister Jacques Parizeau in the National Assembly on September 7, 1995, which would grant the National Assembly of Quebec the power to proclaim that Quebec will become a sovereign country without the need to follow the amending procedure provided for in Part V of the *Constitution Act, 1982*, constitutes a serious threat to the rights and freedoms of the plaintiff guaranteed by the *Canadian Charter of Rights and Freedoms*, in particular ss. 2, 3, 6, 7, 15, and 24(1)[.][21]

In his press conference following the judgment of the Superior Court, the Attorney General of Quebec commented:

Il [the Court] prétend que ça ne sera pas en conformité avec la constitution canadienne. Alors, moi je vous dis que à ce moment-là, l'ordre international intervient et que c'est une question de reconnaissance et

---

[18] *Id.*, at p. 428.

[19] *Id.*, at p. 431.

[20] *Id.*, at p. 432.

[21] *Ibid.*; *quare* whether the adapted declaration entirely respected the logic of the reasoning of the rest of the judgment, which was directed towards a draft bill, not a bill.

c'est ce que nous soumettons depuis toujours. [...] [P]ar la suite, l'effet de ça, l'effet que les Québécois auront dit oui, peut entraîner une rupture avec la constitution canadienne. Ben oui, on l'a toujours déclaré et c'est un effet, et je dirais, souhaité et voulu dans le sens que par la suite, on propose au Canada, on tend la main pour un partenariat économique mais, par contre, le Québec est, lui, devenu un pays.[22]

The *Singh* Case

On October 23, 1995, a motion for declaratory judgment in the Superior Court of Quebec was filed by Stephen Scott, a professor of constitutional law at McGill University, on behalf of Dr. Roopnarine Singh and others, challenging the validity of Bill 1 and any similar measures. The petitioners did not seek to interfere with the holding of the referendum, but in light of the apparent refusal of the Government of Quebec to respect the judgment of Lesage J. concerning the threat to the Constitution posed by Bill 1, it was, in their view, "therefore necessary to obtain a final declaratory order [...] in the most explicit and categorical terms" that Bill 1, if enacted, would be *ultra vires* and of no force and effect. While such a ruling on a bill would normally be premature, it was warranted, the petitioners argued, by the fact that Bill 1, "in its object, scale and scope," amounted to "a total and flagrant assault upon the Constitution, including the status of the courts of law," and because it was clear that the bill was in fact intended, through its sweeping character and in the event of an affirmative referendum vote, to create "an irresistible revolutionary momentum".[23]

The Referendum

On October 30, 1995, the Government of Quebec held the referendum. The electors of Quebec were asked, in accordance with the question tabled with Bill 1 and adopted by the National Assembly, whether they agreed that Quebec "should become sovereign" after having made an offer to Canada for a new economic and political partnership, within the scope of Bill 1 and the tripartite agreement of June 12, 1995. On the same day, the Deputy Premier of Quebec and Minister of International Affairs, Immigration and Cultural Communities, Mr. Bernard Landry, sent letters to representatives of various foreign countries commenting upon the process leading up to the referendum and asking that their countries publicly take note of the referendum results. In his letter, the Deputy Premier wrote:

> Une fois le résultat connu, il apparaîtra opportun que la communauté internationale, et plus particulièrement le pays que vous représentez, prenne acte publiquement de la volonté que les Québécoises et les

---

[22] Transcript of press conference held by the Attorney General of Quebec, Mr. Paul Bégin (8 September 1995), filed of record by the Attorney General of Canada in the *Quebec Secession Reference*; Case, vol. III, tab 26 at pp. 636–637, 639.

[23] *Singh et al. v. Attorney General of Quebec* (23 October 1995), Montreal 500-05-11275-953 (Sup. Ct.); a copy of the motion for declaratory judgment was filed of record by the Attorney General of Canada in the *Quebec Secession Reference*; Case, vol. IV, tab 28, at p. 57.

Québécois auront démocratiquement exprimée relativement à leur avenir.

Puis lorsque l'Assemblée nationale du Québec aura proclamé la souveraineté du nouvel État, le moment sera venu de le reconnaître, sans que ce geste mette en péril de bons rapports avec le reste du Canada.[24]

This early quest for the beginnings of international recognition is reflected in Premier Parizeau's later writings setting out the strategy to be pursued.[25]

The "geste solennel" contemplated by Mr. Parizeau would not be an immediate U.D.I., but neither was a U.D.I. ruled out.[26] According to Premier Bouchard's office, the day after a YES vote, the National Assembly would have been convened in order to adopt the following motion:

L'Assemblée nationale, conformément au vote majoritaire du peuple du Québec, affirme que le Québec deviendra souverain, après que le gouvernement du Québec aura, dans les meilleurs délais, offert formellement au Canada un nouveau partenariat économique et politique, dans le cadre du projet de loi sur l'avenir du Québec et de l'entente signée le 12 juin 1995. La négociation du partenariat et l'accession du Québec à la souveraineté se feront conformément aux dispositions du projet de loi sur l'avenir du Québec.[27]

---

[24] Letter sent by the Deputy Premier of Quebec (30 October 1995), filed of record by the Attorney General of Canada in the *Quebec Secession Reference*; Case, addendum I, at p. 2.

[25] "À l'occasion d'une visite officielle en France en janvier 1995 [...] Valéry Giscard d'Estaing a soulevé une question dont je n'avais pas, jusque-là, compris la portée. Il faut, disait-il en substance, dès la victoire du OUI au référendum, dans les heures ou les jours qui suivent, qu'un geste solennel soit accompli par le Québec pour proclamer sa souveraineté. Sans cela, aucune reconnaissance rapide, c'est-à-dire dans la semaine ou les dix jours suivants, n'est possible de la part d'un pays étranger. Que l'on suspende, pendant disons six mois ou un an, l'application de la proclamation d'indépendance pour donner le temps à des négociations avec le Canada d'aboutir ou pour rédiger conjointement avec le Canada un traité de partenariat, fort bien. Seulement la France, comme les autres pays du monde du reste, ne peut reconnaître qu'un pays. Elle ne reconnaît pas une intention." Jacques Parizeau, *Pour un Québec souverain*, *op. cit.*, p. 286.

[26] *Ibid.* Mr. Parizeau's intentions, as expressed in his book, appear, at best, to be ambiguous and open to interpretation. For example, it is in the next paragraph that he underscored the fact that he had never ruled out a U.D.I. in any of his public and private statements. In his press release of May 8, 1997, he clarified that in the days following a YES victory, he would have proceeded either with an Act, or a motion of the National Assembly, affirming that Quebec would become sovereign. He added that either scenario was compatible with Bill 1 and the June 12, 1996 agreement to negotiate a partnership with Canada. Even here, however, Mr. Parizeau chose to note that a U.D.I. was an integral part of both Bill 1 and the June 12th agreement.

[27] "Processus d'accession à la souveraineté: le rappel des faits," press release of the Office of the Premier of Quebec (7 May 1997); filed of record by the Attorney General of Canada in the *Quebec Secession Reference*; Case, addendum II, tab 1, p. 1. *Quare* whether Bill 1 would have later been adopted by the National Assembly or enacted by the legislature of Quebec or whether, to avoid a further challenge before the courts in the pending *Singh* case and the *Bertrand* main action, the Bill would have continued to remain in limbo, guiding the actions of the Government and the National Assembly in negotiating a partnership treaty and/or in proclaiming sovereignty unilaterally in the event of a failure in negotiations, without ever becoming a (purported) Act, prior to an actual declaration of independence.

Whatever may have been the actual intent of the Government of Quebec in the days and months following a YES vote in the referendum, under Quebec's *Referendum Act* and as a matter of constitutional law, a referendum is and can only be an advisory or "consultative" mechanism. The federal government's failure to appear and join in the *Bertrand* and *Singh* litigation and its participation in the October 1995 referendum was later criticized by some as a breach of the federal government's duty to oppose an "illegal" referendum, i.e., one aimed at subverting the application of the Constitution of Canada by illegal means.[28]

But while there is a legal duty to refrain from engaging in illegal action, why would participation in a referendum (which, as a matter of law, is not binding) be a violation of that duty? The answer, according to this argument, is because it was the clear intention of the Government of Quebec to treat that referendum as a *decision* authorizing a unilateral declaration of independence, and the federal government, by participating in the process, had held itself out as accepting the result and was therefore complicit in the threat of illegal action by the government and National Assembly of Quebec.

In the October 1995 referendum, the Government of Quebec sought to sanction an essentially *unilateral* process by which Quebec's sovereignty would be proclaimed by the National Assembly within one year. While an offer of negotiations with the Government of Canada would have been made, those negotiations would have had the object of securing a partnership treaty between sovereign states and settling other issues such as the apportionment of debts and assets, in accordance with a time-frame and conditions leading to the secession of Quebec from Canada determined by the government and National Assembly of the province. The October 1995 referendum was a means of attempting to legitimize, through the democratic principle, a unilateral secession that would be illegal under the Constitution of Canada.

What such an argument misses, however, as the Attorney General of Canada later submitted in the Reference, is that it is both the prerogative and the responsibility of the Government of Canada to exercise its judgment in accordance with its assessment of the prevailing political environment at any given time. A whole host of variables must be taken into account in developing and adjusting that assessment from day to day. It was within the federal government's purview to determine that, for the time being, a litigation strategy was ill-advised; that the better approach was to continue to place the burden on the sovereigntists to explain *why*

---

[28] For example, Guy Bertrand submitted in his factum (para. 124) in the *Quebec Secession Reference* that "le gouvernement canadien a gravement manqué à ses obligations et à ses devoirs constitutionnels, lors du dernier référendum d'octobre 1995 et par la suite jusqu'à ce jour, en omettant ou négligeant de s'opposer et de contester toute tentative du gouvernement du Québec de détruire unilatéralement la constitution canadienne."

the break-up of Canada would benefit Quebecers, rather than to focus on technical questions about *how* secession might be accomplished.[29]

On October 30, 1995, the referendum result was 50.58% for the NO side and 49.42% for the YES side.[30] Both Premier Parizeau and Mr. Bouchard predicted that there would be another sovereignty referendum in the not-too-distant future.[31]

Federal Government Initiatives

On November 27, 1995, less than a month after the referendum, the Prime Minister of Canada announced three initiatives for change in furtherance of commitments he made during the referendum campaign. The Government of Canada tabled a motion in both Houses of Parliament to recognize Quebec as a distinct society within Canada that includes a French-speaking majority, a unique culture, and a tradition of civil law. The Minister of Justice introduced a bill to require the consent of Quebec, Ontario, the Atlantic, and the Western regions of the country before any general constitutional amendment could be proposed by a Minister of the Government of Canada in the Senate or the House of Commons. As well, the Minister of Human Resources Development would, in reforming the unemployment insurance program, adopt an approach that would defer to provincial jurisdiction in the field of education and the role of the provincial governments in labour-market training.[32]

---

[29] It is not for the courts to pass judgment on the wisdom of such an approach. Nor should the courts preclude the federal government from determining whether and to what degree to participate in a future referendum campaign in Quebec; provided that the federal government conducts itself in accordance with the principle that a referendum is a consultative measure. Resort is often had to the discourse of duties and obligations to justify or to explain why a particular course of action has been adopted. While the general duty to uphold the Constitution and the rule of law certainly supported the later action of the Attorney General of Canada in intervening in the *Bertrand* case, it cannot be true that conversely, had the Attorney General of Canada chosen not to have counsel appear in the *Bertrand* proceedings (and opted instead for another course of action, such as, for example, awaiting developments in the *Singh* case, or an appeal in *Bertrand*), he would have been in breach of his duty. Rather, the means of satisfying the general duty must be left to the discretion of the Attorney General and the Government of Canada.

[30] *Rapport des résultats officiels du scrutin: référendum du 30 octobre 1995*, Chief Electoral Officer of Quebec, November 1995.

[31] "Gardons espoir, gardons l'espoir car la prochaine fois sera la bonne! Et elle pourra venir, cette prochaine fois, elle pourrait venir plus rapidement qu'on le pense." Speech of Mr. Bouchard (30 October 1995). "On était si proches du pays, bon ben c'est retardé un peu. Pas longtemps. On n'attendra pas quinze ans, cette fois-là. Non." Speech of Mr. Parizeau (30 October 1995). Filed of record in the *Quebec Secession Reference; Case*, vol. IV, tab 30 at 700.

[32] The House resolutions on Quebec's distinct society were adopted by the Commons on December 11, 1995 and by the Senate on December 14, 1995. Bill C-110, *An Act respecting constitutional amendments*, the "regional veto bill," was amended to specify British Columbia as a fifth region. The legislation received royal assent on February 2, 1996. (S.C. 1996, c. 1.) The Bloc Québécois and the Reform Party both opposed the adoption of the resolutions and the enactment of the legislation, respectively.

The Speech from the Throne opening Parliament on February 27, 1996 conveyed a positive vision for the unity of the country. However, it also reflected the Government of Canada's determination to deal squarely with the possibility of secession, and to ensure that henceforth, frankness and clarity would be brought to the discussion:

> The Government intends to focus its energies on positive action to prepare Canada for the 21st century. The Government welcomes the commitment of the new government of Quebec to focus all its energies on the real problems of its citizens. The Government will work in collaboration with the Government of Quebec and all provincial governments on an agenda of economic renewal and job creation.
>
> But as long as the prospect of another Quebec referendum exists, the Government will exercise its responsibility to ensure that the debate is conducted with all the facts on the table, that the rules of the process are fair, that the consequences are clear, and that all Canadians, no matter where they live, will have a say in the future of their country.[33]

Motions to Dismiss the *Bertrand* and *Singh* Cases

In the meantime, on January 3, 1996, Mr. Guy Bertrand had filed a revised action for declaratory judgment and permanent injunction, re-amending his initial action of August 10, 1995.[34] On April 12, 1996, the Attorney General of Québec filed a motion to dismiss the *Bertrand* action, and on April 30, 1996, a virtually identical motion to dismiss the *Singh* case.[35]

The Attorney General of Quebec sought to argue, *inter alia*, that the issues raised by the plaintiffs were "non-justiciables." The motion to dismiss went on to allege that

> [l]e recours du demandeur est également irrecevable parce que le processus d'accession du Québec à la souveraineté relève essentiellement d'une démarche démocratique fondamentale qui trouve sa sanction dans le droit international public et la Cour supérieure n'a pas juridiction à cet égard.
>
> Le pouvoir judiciaire n'a pas à intervenir relativement à la question du processus d'accession du Québec à la souveraineté, l'opportunité de ce processus n'ayant pas à être débattue devant les tribunaux.[36]

---

[33] Speech from the Throne to open the Second Session of the Thirty-Fifth Parliament, *House of Commons Debates* (27 February 1996), vol. 133, p. 5. The pursuit of this two-pronged policy was simplistically reduced by media shorthand to a "Plan A" (national reconciliation) and "Plan B" (rules of secession) approach, although there was never any "Plan A" or "Plan B" as such, but rather a concerted effort to deal with the unity challenges facing the country in both a positive and a fully realistic manner. The somewhat dubious distinction of first coining the use of the "Plan B" terminology in the secession context probably belongs to Gordon Gibson, who published an analysis in 1994 entitled *Plan B: The Future of the Rest of Canada* (Vancouver: Fraser Institute). For another example, see *Coming to Terms with Plan B: Ten Principles Governing Secession*, by Patrick Monahan and Michael Bryant (Toronto: C.D. Howe Institute, 1996).

[34] *Bertrand v. Bégin* (3 January 1996), Quebec 200-05-002117-955 (Superior Ct.).

[35] *Bertrand v. Bégin* (12 April 1996), declinatory motion and motion to dismiss; *Singh v. Attorney General of Quebec* (30 April 1996), Montréal: 500-05-011275-933 (Superior Ct.).

[36] Motion to dismiss, *supra*, paras. 4, 12, 13.

It would be difficult to over-emphasize the impact of the position advanced by the Attorney General of Quebec. The Attorney General of Quebec's position was *not* simply that this particular case was moot with respect to Bill 1 and the previous referendum, or premature and hypothetical in regard to a future referendum and new sovereignty legislation or similar measures; it was that the Superior Court of Quebec would *never* have any jurisdiction over the secession process. This was a bald assertion that the Government of Quebec's "process of accession to sovereignty" was wholly and forever outside the jurisdiction of the Constitution and the courts of Canada, and was approved by international law. On May 3, 1996, the Attorney General of Canada stated in response to a question in the House of Commons that the federal government was considering the question of participating in the hearing before the Superior Court on the motion to dismiss. "I would, however, like to point out," the Minister stated, "that our reason for this is not connected with the positions of either Mr. Bertrand or Mr. Singh, but rather the position taken by the Government of Quebec." He added later:

> Primarily, the question under consideration is the position taken by the government of Quebec that the Canadian constitution and the courts are absolutely without a role in the question of a declaration of sovereignty. That's an extraordinary position, and we're currently studying the implications of that position.[37]

On May 10, 1996, the Honourable Allan Rock announced that counsel would appear on his behalf at the hearing of the motion to dismiss the *Bertrand* action.[38]

Urgent Motion in the National Assembly

The hearing of the motion to dismiss began on May 13, 1996, in Quebec City. On May 14, 1996, the Premier of Quebec, Mr. Lucien Bouchard (who had succeeded Mr. Parizeau as Premier on January 29, 1996), suspended the National Assembly's rules of procedure to table an urgent motion relating to self-determination and Quebec's future political status. The National Assembly adopted the motion on May 22, 1996. The Official Opposition voted against the motion. During the course of his speech on the motion, Premier Bouchard stated:

> Notre premier choix est donc d'accéder à la souveraineté après avoir défini un partenariat avec le Canada dans un processus mutuellement acceptable. Nous ajoutons cependant que, si le Canada rejette notre main tendue, si le Canada veut nous imposer des veto, nous retenir dans la Fédération contre notre gré, nous allons nous en retirer en proclamant unilatéralement notre souveraineté. C'est notre droit, nous allons l'exercer.

---

[37] The Hon. Allan Rock, *House of Commons Debates* (May 3, 1996) [translation], vol. 134, no. 39, at p. 2306. "Quebec's Court Stand Is Out of Line, Rock Says"; *The Gazette* (4 May 1996).

[38] News release, Attorney General of Canada, "Federal Government to Respond to Quebec's Position in Court Case" (10 May 1996); *Quebec Secession Reference*; Case, vol. V, tab 39 at p. 910.

[ ] La prochaine fois que le gouvernement des Québécois, la prochaine fois que l'Assemblée nationale reviendra sur cette question de notre droit à disposer de nous-mêmes, ce ne sera pas pour le discuter ou pour le réaffirmer, ce sera pour l'exercer.[39]

The Position of the Attorney General of Canada

On the same day that the Premier of Quebec was speaking in the National Assembly, counsel were pleading the position of the Attorney General of Canada before the Superior Court of Quebec. The Attorney General of Canada's intervention was limited to assisting the Court in its examination of two key issues raised by the Attorney General of Quebec's motion:

(1) the relevance of the Constitution of Canada and the rule of law to any process aimed at changing the constitutional status of Quebec, and the role of the courts in protecting the principles underlying the Constitution and the rule of law;

(2) the jurisdiction of the courts—and, in particular, the Superior Court of Quebec—to determine the validity of any measure which purports to make legally binding and give the force of law to a declaration to the effect that Quebec is no longer a province of Canada but rather a separate and independent sovereign state.[40]

The Attorney General of Canada's position was articulated on the basis of the following guiding principles and postulates relating to the Constitution of Canada, the rule of law and the role of the courts:

Canada is a constitutional democracy. Its political institutions are subject to fundamental rules which govern the conduct of all actors, including governments and legislatures, and which forbid the exercise of arbitrary powers. No one is above the law. All are subject to the rule of law. The courts are the guardians of the Constitution and the rule of law.

The role and powers of the provincial superior courts are essential to the preservation of the rule of law. It is manifestly the prerogative and duty of the courts, as defenders of the Constitution, to ensure that the principles of this supreme law are respected. It follows that the validity of any bill, if enacted—or any similar measure to which the legislature or government purports to give binding legal effect—may be tested before the courts. If the measure is found to be inconsistent with the provisions of the Constitution, the courts will declare it to be *ultra vires* or of no force or effect.[41]

---

[39] "Motion proposant que l'Assemblée réaffirme la liberté du Québec de déterminer son statut politique," Quebec, National Assembly, *Journal des débats*, vols. 35-20, 35-24 (14, 21, 22 May 1996), and esp. pp. 1247, 1248. The English version of the motion read: "THAT the National Assembly reaffirm that the people of Québec are free to take charge of their own destiny, to define without interference their political status and to ensure their economic, social and cultural development." See National Assembly, *Votes and Proceedings* (22 May 1996), no. 24.

[40] *Bertrand v. Bégin, supra*; Synopsis of the Position of the Attorney General of Canada on the Motion to Dismiss, May 22, 1996, p. 2, para. 6.

[41] *Ibid.* (Excerpted from paras. 8–12 of the Synopsis.) See notably: *Amax Potash Ltd. v. Saskatchewan*, [1977] 2 S.C.R. 576, at p. 590 (*per* Dickson J.); *Re: Manitoba Language*

In exercising their discretion whether to deal with a matter that is alleged to be non-justiciable, the courts' primary concern must be focused on retaining their proper role "within the constitutional framework of our democratic form of government."[42] The Attorney General of Canada submitted that important issues of substance existed that were, "at least in part, constitutional in character" and that had "a sufficient legal component to warrant the intervention of the judicial branch."[43] These substantive issues were clearly within the inherent jurisdiction of the Superior Court, and in light of the role of the courts and the importance of the issues, the Court should, it was argued, exercise its discretion to allow the case to proceed to trial on the merits.

The Attorney General of Quebec's motion to dismiss the *Bertrand* case relied, *inter alia*, on international instruments and on public international law, which, it was claimed by the Attorney General of Quebec, sanctioned the "process of accession of Quebec to sovereignty." However, the Attorney General of Canada was of the contrary view: neither international law nor Canadian constitutional law conferred on the National Assembly of Quebec a right of unilateral secession; while secession is not expressly prohibited in international law, Quebec does not meet the conditions for a right to secede. Disagreement on this crucial issue itself was sufficient to demonstrate, in the view of the Attorney General of Canada, that there were substantive *legal* issues in the case that were justiciable in the Superior Court of Quebec.

> The Attorney General of Canada does not challenge the right of Quebecers to express democratically their desire to secede or to stay in Canada. However, the secession of any province would need to be done in accordance with the rule of law. The rule of law is not an obstacle to change; rather, it provides the framework within which change can occur in an orderly fashion.[44]

The Judgment of Mr. Justice Pidgeon in the *Bertrand* Case

On August 30, 1996, the Superior Court ruled on the motion to dismiss. In rendering his decision on the motion, Mr. Justice Robert Pidgeon prefaced his findings with a discursive analysis of the role of the courts in protecting the rule of law.

> The principle of the rule of law is the cornerstone of our democratic system. Incorporated in the preamble of the *Charter*, it guarantees

---

Rights, [1985] 1 S.C.R. 721, at p. 745; *Roncarelli v. Duplessis*, [1959] S.C.R. 121, at p. 142 (*per* Rand J.); *MacMillan Bloedel Ltd. v. Simpson*, [1995] 4 S.C.R. 725, at pp. 753–754 (*per* Lamer C.J.C.).

[42] *Id.*, para. 14 of the Synopsis. *Re: Canada Assistance Plan (B.C.)*, [1991] 2 S.C.R. 525 (*per* Sopinka J.).

[43] *Id.*, para. 19. The words are from the test formulated by Sopinka J. in *Re: Canada Assistance Plan (B.C.)*, *supra*.

[44] *Ibid.* (Taken from paras. 14–18 of the Synopsis.)

citizens that their fundamental rights will be respected irrespective of their origin, race, colour, religion or language. To ensure its maintenance, there is an independent institution sheltered from all constraint or influence by the executive, the legislature, pressure groups, public opinion and even the media. Its duty is to ensure that everyone, including governments, abides by the laws and that the actions of some do not infringe the rights of others. *This institution is the judiciary.*[45]

In Quebec, Pidgeon J. noted, this institution "is the Superior Court, a provincial court of general jurisdiction, which, since its establishment in 1849 [...] has had as its primary mission the maintenance of the rule of law."[46]

The Court examined the five basic arguments advanced by the Attorney General of Quebec in favour of dismissal of the action:

1. parliamentary immunity;

2. the strictly political nature of the argument;

3. the consistency of the initiative with international law;

4. the strictly hypothetical nature of the question; and

5. the failure to adopt the French version of certain documents in the schedules to the *Constitution Act, 1982.*[47]

In extensive reasons for judgment, the Court rejected each and every one of the grounds advanced for dismissal. With respect to the parliamentary immunity argument, Pidgeon J. stated that "the issue raised by the plaintiff, namely, that the Government of Quebec cannot rely on parliamentary immunity to evade the Constitution of Canada, the source of its powers, in order to accomplish its plan for unilateral secession, raises an issue that ought to be referred to the judge in the main action."[48]

---

[45] *Bertrand c. Bégin,* [1996] R.J.Q. 2393 (emphasis in original). The citations in this book are drawn from the English translation of the decision in the Dominion Law Reports, reported as *Bertrand v. Quebec (Attorney General),* 138 D.L.R. (4th) 481; at pp. 491–492.

[46] *Id.,* at p. 492.

[47] This latter ground was not part of the original motion to dismiss the *Bertrand* case filed with the Court on April 12, 1996, and was raised orally and *in extremis* by counsel for the Attorney General of Quebec on May 15, 1996. Permission to amend the motion was granted by the Court, and a further exchange of pleadings and a hearing on this issue took place in June 1996. The Court denied this ground in its judgment of August 30, 1996 (see reasons of Pidgeon J. at pp. 509–512). That the absence of an official French language version of certain constitutional instruments does not result in the invalidity or inoperativity of the Constitution of Canada itself was confirmed in later decisions of the Court of Quebec, the Superior Court, and the Court of Appeal of Quebec. This issue is extraneous to the question of the secession of Quebec from Canada and will not be dealt with in this book. See Warren J. Newman, "The Duty to Prepare and Put Forward for Enactment the French-Language Version of Certain Constitutional Instruments: From the *Bertrand* Case to the *Langlois* Case," Conference Paper delivered at the National Symposium on Canada's Official Languages to mark the 10th Anniversary of the *Official Languages Act* of 1988; Ottawa Congress Centre, September 16 to 18, 1998. The paper is also available in French.

[48] *Id.,* at p. 500.

With regard to the argument that the process of accession to sovereignty is an essentially political initiative that is not subject to judicial review, the Court noted that "the plaintiff refers to a threat that several of his fundamental rights guaranteed by sections 2, 3, 6, 7, 15, 16, and 24(1) of the *Charter* will be violated." In the face of such allegations, which would support some of the conclusions of the action, and with the state of the law unclear, Pidgeon J. stated, "I have no choice but to refer the matter to the judge in the main action."[49]

On the question of the application of international law, the Court "must determine whether the issue is indeed covered in international law and whether this law is applicable in the instant case. Here again, there is a significant controversy."[50] Pidgeon J. added:

> Once the international law has been substantiated, the Court will have to determine whether it prevails over the domestic law. The two questions are indissociable.

As to the allegedly hypothetical nature of the question, counsel for the Attorney General of Quebec had argued that the question before the Court was moot. Unlike the situation that had prevailed when Lesage J. rendered his earlier judgment, the referendum was over and Bill 1 had died on the order paper. Pidgeon J. summarized the examples given by the Attorney General of Quebec, demonstrating that the Court was faced with a purely hypothetical situation, as follows:

> When will the elections be held? Who will the people vote for? Will the government decide to hold a referendum? What will it be on? On a question, or a bill? What will be the content of the question or bill? Will there be, as there was in 1995, a partnership proposal? Will there be some negotiations? For how long? Will they result in a total or partial agreement?[51]

Mr. Justice Pidgeon was not prepared to dismiss the case as being purely hypothetical.

> I agree that some of the issues raised by the plaintiff have become moot. The fact that *Bill 1 respecting the future of Québec* died on the order paper means that the conclusions dealing with it are moot.
>
> However, while some of the questions submitted may appear hypothetical or theoretical to the defendant, their consequences are highly practical for the plaintiff. For example, he alleges that the Quebec government might deprive him of some of his fundamental rights such as the right to be able to reside, travel and work anywhere in Canada.[52]

Moreover, the Court took judicial notice of the passage by the National Assembly of the urgent resolution on self-determination during the course

---

[49] *Id.*, at pp. 501–502.
[50] *Id.*, at p. 502.
[51] *Id.*, at p. 506.
[52] *Id.*, at p. 507.

of hearing of the Attorney General of Quebec's motion to dismiss, which tended to support the plaintiff's allegation that "this plan is still alive."

> In any event, even if all the questions raised by the action were purely hypothetical, it would still be advisable to refer the matter to the judge trying the matter on its merits.
>
> The latter, hearing a hypothetical case raising constitutional issues involving allegations of a violation or threatened violation of *Charter* rights, has a discretionary latitude that is lacking in a court hearing a motion to dismiss.

Mr. Justice Pidgeon identified the following issues as "some of the constitutional issues raised by the plaintiff [that] deserve a determination on the merits":

• Is the right to self-determination synonymous with the right to secession?

• Can Quebec unilaterally secede from Canada?

• Is Quebec's process for achieving sovereignty consistent with international law?

• Does international law prevail over domestic law?[53]

On September 4, 1996, the Attorney General of Quebec announced at a press conference that the Government of Quebec would no longer participate in the *Bertrand* case. Mr. Bégin stated:

> [A]près avoir prétendu, suivi nos propositions pendant deux reprises devant le juge Lesage et devant le juge Pidgeon à l'effet qu'il ne revenait pas aux tribunaux de se prononcer et après avoir reçu deux décisions à cet égard, nous avons décidé de ne pas porter en appel cette décision et de ne pas être présent devant la Cour lorsque le dossier continuera devant le juge Pidgeon ou un autre juge qui sera désigné par le juge en chef.[54]

---

[53] *Id.*, at pp. 507–508. The "constitutional issues" identified by Pidgeon J. later formed the basis for the questions submitted by the Governor in Council for hearing and consideration in the *Quebec Secession Reference*.

[54] Transcript of press conference held by the Attorney General of Quebec (4 September 1996), filed of record in the *Quebec Secession Reference*, Case, vol. V, tab 42, at p. 991.

3

The Reference Proceedings and the Court's Opinion

Announcement of the Reference to the Supreme Court

The decision of the Attorney General of Quebec not to participate in the hearing on the merits of the *Bertrand* case before the Superior Court—yet all the while maintaining that courts in Canada had no jurisdiction over the Quebec government's secession process and that international law was the only relevant body of law—meant that the *Bertrand* case was unlikely to be a successful vehicle for obtaining an early, authoritative, and definitive judicial ruling on the controversy. The Superior Court would be deprived of the benefit of hearing the other side of the case, in the absence of counsel for the Attorney General of Quebec. And if Mr. Bertrand won his case, there would be virtually no likelihood of an appeal and further consideration of the issues by a higher court, because the Government of Quebec had adamantly refused to recognize the jurisdiction of the courts in any event. But Mr. Justice Pidgeon of the Superior Court had identified a number of very tangible and important legal issues that needed to be determined.

On September 26, 1996, the Minister of Justice and the Attorney General of Canada, Mr. Allan Rock, wrote to his Quebec counterpart, Mr. Paul Bégin, to explain the reasons that motivated the Government of Canada's decision to announce that it would submit a reference to the Supreme Court of Canada concerning certain questions relating to the unilateral secession of Quebec from Canada, having regard to the issues formulated by Mr. Justice Pidgeon. Mr. Rock wrote as follows:

> The Governments of Quebec and of Canada are in disagreement over a process so serious that it could lead to the secession of Quebec. Other provincial governments have also stated points of view that are different from that of the Government of Quebec. The Government of Quebec submits that it can determine by itself alone the process of secession and that it is supported in this by international law. The federal government submits that international law does not give this power to the Government of Quebec and that a referendum does not create, as a matter of law, an automatic right of secession.
>
> There are above all—which is even more dangerous—profound disagreements between citizens on the whole question as to which process to follow. As responsible governments, we have the duty to ensure that this crucial question is clarified. We need to know the state of Canadian domestic law, of international law, and which of them takes priority.
>
> I understand the Government of Quebec deems it inappropriate to continue this debate within the framework of the *Bertrand* case. However,

Mr. Justice Pidgeon had identified the fundamental issues that must be clarified if we want to deal with any process related to the future of Quebec and Canada on a foundation that is stable, fair and respectful of the rule of law. It is on the basis of this judgment of the Superior Court of Quebec that I have formulated the three questions that I will refer to the Supreme Court.[1]

That same day, the Minister of Justice rose in the House of Commons to announce his intention "to refer to the Supreme Court of Canada certain specific questions of great importance to all Canadians." In a wide-ranging and often philosophical statement that reflected both his eloquence and his deep conviction,[2] Mr. Rock spoke to the values shared by all Canadians— Quebecers included—and how those values were being put at risk by the position of the Government of Quebec in relation to a future referendum and the possibility of a U.D.I.

On two occasions in the recent past the majority of Quebecers have voted for a united Canada. Notwithstanding those democratic expressions of the popular will, the current government of the province of Quebec seems determined to bring the issue to a third vote at some future time. Moreover, it claims to be entitled to make a unilateral declaration of independence to create a separate state of Quebec. In our view that position is contrary to Canadian law, is unsupported by international law and is deeply threatening to the orderly governance of our nation. [...]

The Government of Quebec has expressly stated that the Constitution and the courts have no role to play in determining the correctness of its position. As we have argued in court and as I have asserted here in the House, we believe its position to be profoundly wrong.

To leave this issue unresolved would pose a serious threat to orderly government in Quebec and in the rest of Canada.

The Minister stressed that the Government of Canada was not challenging the capacity of the Government of Quebec to consult the population through a referendum, but that the outcome of a referendum could not, without more, change the legal status of a province. Moreover, a referendum vote alone could never form the justification for a unilateral declaration of independence in a country like Canada, one of the few countries in the world where the possibility of secession has been admitted.

The Government of Canada does not argue against the legitimacy of a consultative referendum. A referendum is an opportunity for a government to consult with the people. But however important that consultation may be, the result of a referendum does not in and of itself effect legal change.

---

[1] Letter of Minister of Justice and Attorney General of Canada to Attorney General of Quebec (26 September 1996) [translation], filed of record in the *Quebec Secession Reference*, Case, vol. V, tab 43 at pp. 1003, 1004.

[2] Statement by the Hon. Allan Rock, Minister of Justice and Attorney General of Canada, *House of Commons Debates* (26 September 1996) vol. 134, no. 75, at pp. 4707–4711.

It is terribly important to remember that in the Canadian context there is no political justification to argue for a unilateral declaration of independence by the Quebec National Assembly.

In most countries the very idea of secession would be rejected. But that has not been so in Canada. There have been two referenda in Quebec. The leading political figures of all the provinces and indeed the Canadian public have long agreed that this country will not be held together against the will of Quebecers clearly expressed. And this government agrees with that statement.

This position arises partly out of our traditions of tolerance and mutual respect but also because we know instinctively that the quality and the functioning of our democracy requires the broad consent of all Canadians.

A U.D.I. would run completely counter to Canada's tradition of evolution, not revolution, and the importance, in a civilized state, of promoting stability, legal continuity, and orderly transition.

A unilateral declaration of independence would undermine political stability, interrupt the prevailing order and cast into doubt the interests and rights of Quebecers and all Canadians.

A unilateral declaration of independence would create the most serious difficulties for ordinary Quebecers. There would be wide-spread uncertainty within Quebec about which legal regime was effectively in control. [...]

The issue is not just a mere legal nicety. It is also of enormous practical significance. Any government that suggests it would throw Quebec and all of Canada into the confusion of a unilateral declaration of independence is being profoundly irresponsible. It is a formula for chaos.

Should the day ever come when the secession of Quebec might have to be envisaged as a reality, "there is no doubt," Mr. Rock emphasized, "that it could only be achieved through negotiation and through agreement."

As I have stressed, our nation is built on shared values of tolerance, accommodation and mutual respect. Canadians are admired throughout the world because of our understanding of the need to accommodate one another to achieve our larger common purposes.

In this respect, we share a commitment to using negotiation and orderly processes to work out differences—something that Canadian individuals and businesses do every day. This commitment is what the international community has come to expect of Canada and to admire.

Canadians' shared values have guided us in the past and will continue to do so in the future. All Canadians, including Quebecers, can take pride in the civility and tolerance we have shown one another in dealing with this fundamental issue. There is every reason to believe that civility will continue.

Our insistence on resolving questions raised by the prospect of Quebec secession through an orderly process and within the framework of law is simply consistent with those values.

The Minister of Justice took great pains to underline the importance to this process of respect for the rule of law, and how this principle works in tandem with another fundamental precept embedded in our constitutional framework, the democratic principle.

> First and foremost, the rule of law, as it has developed in Canada and in other democratic nations around the world, is not simply a legal abstraction or a technical precept. It is a living principle that is fundamental to our democratic way of life. In substance, it means that everyone in our society, including ministers of government, premiers, the rich and powerful and the ordinary citizen alike is governed by the same law of the land. We are all bound by the Constitution, by the Criminal Code, by Acts of Parliament and the legislatures. In cases of dispute regarding the application or interpretation of law, the courts are the ultimate arbiter.
>
> The great value of the rule of law is that it is democratic. Its substance is derived from our democratic institutions. It applies to everyone without qualification. It also permits democracy to flourish because it establishes a stable framework within which the democratic process can work.
>
> The separatist leaders argue that the rule of law is simply a ruse by which the Canadian Government intends to defeat an expression of democratic will by Quebecers—a trick to deny the results of a lost referendum. They argue that to require an orderly process within the legal framework would place Quebec in a straightjacket, defeating the democratic result of a future referendum.
>
> Such arguments are made for political effect. They are based on the misunderstanding that the rule of law and democratic action are somehow mutually exclusive. That is quite wrong. In fact, they coexist in harmony. The safety of both depends upon the integrity of each. The failure to observe either endangers the two at once.
>
> Simply to insist upon an orderly process is not to foreclose the acceptance of change. Let us be vigilant to ensure that the true issue of the day is kept before us. The issue is not whether a democracy such as Canada can keep a population against its will. Of course it cannot. The issue arises from the false claim by the Government of Quebec that it alone, in a unilateral fashion that changes according to its short term political interests, can decide the process that may lead to secession.
>
> Quebecers as well as their fellow citizens across Canada would be dramatically affected by the break-up of our country. Everyone has the right to be certain that the process is lawful, mutually acceptable and fair to all.

Immediately after Mr. Rock's statement, the Attorney General of Quebec, Mr. Bégin, held a press conference at which he maintained his government's position on the role of the courts and the possible recourse to a U.D.I. envisaged by Bill 1.

> Nous avons déclaré depuis le début que ce n'est pas aux tribunaux de décider ce qu'il va advenir. [...]
>
> Je pense que nous avons énoncé très clairement durant la campagne électorale [*sic*] de quelle manière nous entendions procéder. Le texte

prévoyait qu'il y avait des discussions. Après un certain délai, nous espérions avoir conclu un traité de partenariat. Et si c'était devenu impossible, une mécanique était prévue quant à la suite des choses. [...]

Il est prévu que après avoir tenté de négocier pendant une période de temps, l'Assemblée Nationale pourra faire une déclaration. C'est ce qui est écrit dans le projet de loi.[3]

The Reference Questions

On September 30, 1996, the Governor in Council formally submitted the reference questions to the Supreme Court of Canada. The preamble and text of the Order in Council[4] are set out below.

Whereas the Government of Quebec has expressed its view that the National Assembly or government of that province has the right to cause Quebec to secede from Canada unilaterally;

Whereas the Government of Quebec has expressed its view that this right to cause Quebec to secede unilaterally may be acquired in a referendum;

Whereas many Quebecers and other Canadians are uncertain about the constitutional and international situation in the event of a unilateral declaration of independence by the government of Quebec;

Whereas principles of self-determination, popular will, democratic rights and fundamental freedoms, and the rule of law, have been raised in many contexts in relation to the secession of Quebec from Canada;

And whereas the Government of Canada sees fit to refer the matter to the Supreme Court of Canada;

Therefore, His Excellency the Governor in Council, on the recommendation of the Minister of Justice, pursuant to section 53 of the *Supreme Court Act*, hereby submits to the Supreme Court of Canada for hearing and consideration the following questions.

The questions put to the Supreme Court read as follows:

1. Under the Constitution of Canada, can the National Assembly, legislature or government of Quebec effect the secession of Quebec from Canada unilaterally?

2. Does international law give the National Assembly, legislature or government of Quebec the right to effect the secession of Quebec from Canada unilaterally? In this regard, is there a right to self-determination under international law that would give the National Assembly, legislature or government of Quebec the right to effect the secession of Quebec from Canada unilaterally?

3. In the event of a conflict between domestic and international law on the right of the National Assembly, legislature or government

---

[3] Transcript of press conference held by the Attorney General of Quebec (26 September 1996), filed of record in the *Quebec Secession Reference*, Case, vol. V, tab 45, at p. 1026.

[4] P.C. 1996-1497; Case, vol. 1, at p. 1.

of Quebec to effect the secession of Quebec from Canada unilaterally, which would take precedence in Canada?

The Reference Proceedings

In accordance with the *Rules of the Supreme Court of Canada* and orders of the Chief Justice providing additional directions, the Attorney General of Canada was given carriage of the Reference and was made responsible for the preparation and contents of the Case on Appeal (the "Case," in the circumstances of a reference). This consisted of more than five volumes of relevant documentary materials such as the Draft Bill, Bill 1, and the court decisions and public statements relating thereto. The Case would help to provide a factual context to the Court for its consideration of the Reference questions, and was filed by counsel for the Attorney General of Canada on December 27, 1996.

The Attorney General of Canada's factum, consisting of a statement of facts and a series of legal arguments on each of the questions referred to the Court, was filed on February 28, 1997. In addition, the Attorney General of Canada filed an Experts' Report, consisting of a report entitled "State Practice and International Law in relation to Unilateral Secession" by Professor James Crawford, Whewell Professor of International Law at Cambridge University, member of the United Nations International Law Commission and a leading expert on state secession; and a commentary on Professor Crawford's report by Professor Luzius Wildhaber, Professor of International Law at the University of Basel and a judge on the European Court of Human Rights.

The various interveners in the Reference filed their submissions during the course of April 1997. The Attorney General of Canada did not oppose any applications for leave to intervene in the Reference. The interveners were the Attorney General of Manitoba; the Attorney General of Saskatchewan; the Ministers of Justice of the Northwest Territories and the Yukon; Guy Bertrand and Roopnarine Singh *et al.*; the Grand Council of the Cree, Kitigan Zibi Ashinabeg, Makivik Corporation, and the Chiefs of Ontario; the Minority Advocacy Rights Council, the Ad Hoc Committee of Canadian Women on the Constitution; and Vincent Pouliot.[5]

In May 1997, the Court indicated that it would be appointing an *amicus curiae* under s. 53 of the *Supreme Court Act*, which deals with references by the Governor in Council. Subsection 53(7) specifically provides that

---

[5] Guy Bertrand and Roopnarine Singh *et al.* had a direct interest in the Reference because they were plaintiffs in the pending litigation before the Quebec Superior Court. The Grand Council represented the Crees of Quebec; Makivik, the Inuit of Quebec; Kitigan Zibi Ashinabeg, an Algonquin Indian band in the Maniwaki area of Quebec; the Chiefs of Ontario, the Aboriginal Chiefs of that province. The Minority Advocacy Rights Council was based in Toronto and was active in defending and advancing *Charter* equality and minority rights interests, as was the Ad Hoc Committee. Vincent Pouliot was head of the Libertarian Party. Two other interveners, Mi'qmaq Nation, Gespegawagi District, and Yves Michaud, the latter long active in the sovereignty movement in Quebec, later withdrew from the reference proceedings before the hearing took place.

[t]he Court may, in its discretion, request any counsel to argue the case with respect to any interest that is affected and with respect to which counsel does not appear, and the reasonable expenses thereby occasioned may be paid by the Minister of Finance out of any moneys appropriated by Parliament for expenses of litigation.

This decision on the part of the Court was immediately attacked by the Premier and the Deputy Premier of Quebec, who characterized it as an attempt to substitute an "impostor" to argue the Government of Quebec's case.[6] The role of the *amicus curiae*, however, would not be to represent the Government of Quebec, but to assist the Court in examining the other side of the questions. On July 11, 1997, the Court appointed a lawyer from Quebec City, André Joli-Coeur, as *amicus curiae*.[7]

On September 16, 1997, the former Premier of Quebec published an article in which he argued forcefully that the continued willingness of the Government of Quebec to have recourse to a unilateral declaration of independence was "indispensable" to the negotiating strategy of the secessionists.

La meilleure façon d'obtenir l'autorisation du Canada, c'est de ne jamais renoncer, fût-ce un moment, à une déclaration unilatérale de souveraineté. [...] Je ne cesserai pas de penser que sans l'évocation d'une déclaration unilatérale de souveraineté par l'Assemblée nationale, il n'y aura pas de souveraineté.[8]

The current Premier of Quebec stated that he himself could have signed Mr. Parizeau's article.[9] Mr. Bouchard nuanced his position on October 6, 1997 in a speech to the Canadian Alliance of Manufacturers in which he placed the emphasis on negotiating a partnership between Quebec and Canada, without abandoning the possibility of a U.D.I.

And it is only if we do not agree, after making an attempt in good faith, that Quebec's National Assembly will, as a last resort, issue a U.D.I., while taking no steps whatsoever that would undermine our

---

[6] "Un gouvernement du PQ fera outrage à la Cour suprême"; *Le Devoir* (13 May 1997); "Québec ne tiendra aucun compte du jugement de la Cour suprême," *La Presse* (13 May 1997); "Un « jugement politique » que le Québec ignorera"; *Le Droit* (13 May 1997). For an excellent critique of the way in which the Government of Quebec attempted to dissuade members of the Bar of Quebec from accepting the mandate of *amicus curiae* in the *Quebec Secession Reference*, see the article by Maître Pierre Bienvenu entitled "Un dangereux précédent"; *La Presse* (10 November 1998). It was also printed in *Le Journal du Barreau* (1 December 1998) as "À la défense d'un adversaire"; and in English in the Montreal *Gazette* (12 December 1998) under the title "A Dangerous Precedent."

[7] The mandate letter from the Registrar of the Supreme Court to Maître Joli-Coeur read in part: "In this Reference, it would be of assistance to the Court to receive arguments on all sides of these questions and from all points of view. While the Court has before it some arguments supporting an affirmative answer to Questions 1 and 2, it is of the view that it would benefit from additional arguments to that end." (11 July 1997.)

[8] Jacques Parizeau, "La déclaration unilatérale est indispensable"; *Le Devoir* (16 September 1997).

[9] Transcript of a press conference held by Premier Lucien Bouchard (16 September 1997): "Je pourrais signer le texte de M. Parizeau. Je considère que c'est un excellent texte qui est très clair, qui est très transparent et qui pose très bien les choses." Filed of record in the *Quebec Secession Reference*, Case, addendum III, tab 2.

common economic space. [...] But I'm quite sure that U.D.I. will never be necessary. I have faith in the democratic nature of Canada. I have faith in the common economic interests at stake.[10]

These remarks by the former and the current Premier, to the effect that a U.D.I. remained both a lever and an option, were filed by counsel for the Attorney General of Canada as part of the background materials contextualizing the questions in the *Quebec Secession Reference*.

The *amicus curiae* filed his factum in the Reference on December 18, 1997, accompanied by seven experts' reports, in which he challenged the constitutional validity of the jurisdiction of the Court to hear the Reference and, particularly, Question 2 on international law, as well as made substantive arguments in relation to the three questions. Essentially, the *amicus curiae* argued that there was a "principle of effectivity" recognized both in international law and Canadian constitutional law by which Quebec's independence could be effected unilaterally.[11] The Attorney General of Canada filed a reply factum on January 15, 1998 (supported by an experts' reply). Certain of the interveners also filed replies. Maître Joli-Coeur filed a rebuttal and further expert material on February 2, 1998. This included an opinion by Mr. Claude Ryan, the former leader of the Quebec Liberal Party, to the effect that the future of Quebec was a matter to be decided by the sovereign will of the people of Quebec, and that the Supreme Court should refer the questions back to the political actors for democratic responses.

As the hearing date approached, the political campaign against the Reference intensified.[12] The Premier of Quebec, in a speech at the faculty of law of the Université de Montréal, stated:

> Le gouvernement québécois, lui, ne sera pas présent lors de ces audiences. [...] La réponse, c'est la primauté de la démocratie. L'Assemblée Nationale du Québec, le gouvernement des Québécois, sont des émanations de la démocratie québécoise[.]

The federal Minister of Intergovernmental Affairs, the Honourable Stéphane Dion, responded:

> Evidemment, le peuple doit décider, nous sommes en démocratie. Mais qui doit déterminer le processus devant menant à une décision et qui

---

[10] Transcript of a speech by Premier Bouchard to the annual meeting of the Canadian Alliance of Manufacturers (6 October 1997); "Ça passe ou ça casse, dit Bouchard aux gens d'affaires anglophones (Québec recourra à une déclaration unilatérale d'indépendance si les négociations avortent avec le Canada)"; *La Presse* (7 October 1997). *Quebec Secession Reference*, Case, addendum III, tabs 3 and 4.

[11] This *principe d'effectivité* is discussed *infra* in the context of the Court's response to the submissions by the *amicus curiae*. It should be added that on February 6, 1998, the *amicus curiae* filed an addendum to his factum in response to the Court's request that he examine additional arguments based on the international law right of self-determination. Maître Joli-Coeur's conclusion that Quebecers are not an oppressed people was later cited by the Court in its opinion.

[12] "Bouchard dénonce le caractère « colonial » du renvoi fédéral devant la Cour suprême"; "Le dernier mot revient au peuple québécois"; *Le Devoir* (13 February 1998).

doit interpréter le résultat? Il faut une procédure claire, à l'intérieur du cadre juridique, dans le respect de la Constitution et de la loi du pays. [...] Nous croyons que [...] l'histoire de notre pays est exceptionnellement démocratique et que la démarche de sécession unilatérale qu'il envisage serait inacceptable dans toutes des démocraties du monde.[13]

The Quebec Minister for Intergovernmental Affairs repeated the premises of the Government of Quebec's position, to the effect that Quebec's secession process flowed from the international right of self-determination, outside of the Canadian constitutional framework.

La démarche québécoise d'accession à la souveraineté s'inscrit *dans le droit des peuples de disposer de leur avenir* tel que reconnaît la communauté internationale. Elle se situe donc *en dehors du cadre constitutionnel canadien.* Or, Ottawa invoque ce cadre, en particulier la *Loi constitutionelle de 1982,* une loi qu'il voudrait bien voir appliquée au processus québécois d'accession à la souveraineté.[14]

The hearing took place during the week of February 16, 1998, attended by extraordinary media coverage.[15] Counsel for the Attorney General of Canada began the oral argument, followed by the pleadings of the other Attorneys General, the interveners, and the *amicus curiae.* On Thursday, February 19, the Court asked a series of questions directed to either counsel for the Attorney General of Canada or to the *amicus curiae,* or to both. These were responded to orally and then supplemented by written responses filed by the Attorney General of Canada and by the *amicus curiae,* respectively, on March 6, 1998. The Attorney General of Canada filed a reply to the *amicus curiae*'s written responses on March 13, and the *amicus* filed a rebuttal on March 20, 1998. Proceedings in the Reference were closed with a final letter of reply by counsel for the Attorney General of Canada on March 27, 1998.

The Opinion of the Supreme Court in the Reference

The opinion of the Supreme Court was released on August 20, 1998, six months to the day of the closing of oral argument in the case. It was an eloquent, well-reasoned, and balanced response to the issues at the heart of the questions before the Court.

---

[13] "Dion raille le « droit bouchardien »"; *Le Devoir* (13 February 1998).

[14] Déclaration du Ministre délégué aux affaires intergouvernementales canadiennes, M. Jacques Brassard, à l'occasion du début des audiences dans l'affaire du Renvoi devant la Cour suprême (16 February 1998); emphasis added.

[15] E.g., "La cause du siècle"; *La Presse* (16 February 1998); "Get Set for Landmark Case on Legality of UDI": *The Gazette* (14 February 1998); "Showdown in Canada's Supreme Court": *The Ottawa Citizen* (16 February 1998); "Vu l'importance de la cause, la cour posera pour l'Histoire": *Le Devoir* (16 February 1998). Both Newsworld and the Réseau de l'Information (R.D.I.) broadcast the hearings live, with commentary from constitutional law professors, from the lobby of the Supreme Court building.

Jurisdictional and Related Issues

Dealing first with the issues relating to the Court's jurisdiction and discretion to hear the matter, the Court rejected the arguments advanced by the *amicus curiae* that put into question the constitutional validity of s. 53 of the *Supreme Court Act*, as well as the Court's ability to address questions relating to international law. The Court also ruled that the questions put in this reference were justiciable and should be answered by the Court. The position advanced by the Attorney General of Canada on these issues was virtually identical to the finding of the Court.[16]

The constitutional validity of s. 53 of the *Supreme Court Act* turned on whether it was *intra vires* Parliament's power to establish a "general court of appeal" for Canada. Those words, the Court stated, "denote the status of the Court within the national court structure and should not be taken as a restrictive definition of the Court's functions."[17] As to whether a court of appeal may undertake advisory functions, the Court distinguished the situation of the United States Supreme Court, the jurisdiction of which is expressly limited by the U.S. Constitution to actual "cases" or "controversies."[18] The judicial systems in a number of European states do not require the presence of an actual dispute involving the adjudication of rights to review constitutional issues, and the European Court of Justice, the European Court of Human Rights, and the Inter-American Court of Human Rights have the express capacity to render advisory opinions.[19]

Furthermore, there is no strict separation of powers doctrine under the Constitution of Canada.

> Parliament and the provincial legislatures may properly confer other legal functions on the Courts, and may confer certain judicial functions on bodies that are not courts. The exception to this rule relates only to s. 96 courts. Thus, even though the rendering of advisory opinions is quite clearly done outside the framework of adversarial litigation, and such opinions are traditionally obtained by the executive from law officers of the Crown, there is no constitutional bar to this Court's receipt of jurisdiction to undertake such an advisory role. The legislative grant of reference jurisdiction found in s. 53 of the *Supreme Court Act* is therefore constitutionally valid.[20]

With regard to the argument that the questions put in the *Quebec Secession Reference* were beyond the ambit of s. 53 of the *Supreme Court Act*, the Court stated that "[t]his submission cannot be accepted."

---

[16] See Reply factum of the Attorney General of Canada (15 January 1998), paras. 4–24; Reply of the A.G. Canada to Written Responses of the *Amicus Curiae* (13 March 1998), paras. 3–11.

[17] *Reference re Secession of Quebec, supra*; para. 9 of the reasons for judgment.

[18] *Id.*, para. 13.

[19] Para. 14.

[20] Para. 15.

Question 1 is directed, at least in part, to the interpretation of the *Constitution Acts*, which are referred to in s. 53(1)(*a*). Both Question 1 and Question 2 fall within s. 53(1)(*d*), since they relate to the powers of the legislature or government of a Canadian province. Finally, all three questions are clearly "important questions of law or fact concerning any matter" so that they must come within s. 53(2).[21]

Jurisdiction over Question 2

As to the jurisdiction of the Court to address Question 2, the Court noted that it would not, as submitted by the *amicus curiae*, be purporting to act as an international tribunal.

> In accordance with well accepted principles of international law, this Court's answer to Question 2 would not purport to bind any other state or international tribunal that might subsequently consider a similar question. The Court nevertheless has jurisdiction to provide an advisory opinion to the Governor in Council in its capacity as a national court on legal questions touching and concerning the future of the Canadian federation.[22]

The Court also dismissed the *amicus curiae*'s additional concern—that Question 2 was beyond the competence of the Court because it required the Court to consider international law rather than domestic law—as "groundless." The Court had examined international law in a number of previous cases to determine rights and obligations under the Canadian legal system. More to the point, Question 2 did not ask an "abstract question of 'pure' international law." Rather, Question 2 sought to determine the legal rights and obligations of the National Assembly, legislature, or Government of Quebec, "institutions that clearly exist as part of the Canadian legal order."

> [T]he *amicus curiae* himself submitted that the success of any initiative on the part of Quebec to secede from the Canadian federation would be governed by international law. In these circumstances, a consideration of international law in the context of this Reference about the unilateral secession of Quebec is not only permissible but unavoidable.[23]

Justiciability

The *amicus curiae* submitted, in the alternative, that if the Court had *jurisdiction* over the questions referred to it, the Court should exercise its *discretion* not to address them because the questions were not justiciable:

1. because they were too "theoretical" or speculative;

2. because they were political, rather than legal, in nature; and

3. because they were not yet ripe for judicial consideration.

---

[21] Para. 18.

[22] Para. 20.

[23] Paras. 21–23 of the reasons for judgment. For the submissions of the Attorney General of Canada on the Court's jurisdiction as to Question 2, see paras. 16–24 of the Reply factum (15 January 1998).

The Attorney General of Canada argued that the Reference questions were straightforward legal questions and that the Court had been provided with a full documentary record of the relevant events underlying the Reference. This factual context was sufficient to permit a full appreciation of and response to the questions submitted by the Governor in Council. With respect to whether the questions were sufficiently *legal* in nature to be justiciable, the Attorney General of Canada submitted that the facts demonstrated at least the following:

> 1. The Government of Quebec had prepared its proposal to effect the secession of Quebec from Canada in the form of draft *legislation*;
>
> 2. the draft legislation had been the subject of continuous *legal proceedings* before the Superior Court of Quebec;
>
> 3. the Government of Quebec has consistently claimed a *right* to effect unilaterally the secession of Quebec from Canada;
>
> 4. the Superior Court of Quebec has treated the basic legal issues raised by the Draft Bill, Bill 1 and the Government of Quebec's proposed secession process as *justiciable*;
>
> 5. the Government of Quebec has refused to proceed to a trial and to participate in the merits before the Superior Court of Quebec, or to refer the matter to the Court of Appeal; and
>
> 6. the current Government of Quebec remains committed to a process of separating Quebec from Canada that includes possible recourse to a unilateral declaration of independence.[24]

The *amicus curiae* had contended that the facts before the Court were irrelevant because they related to a now-defunct bill and could not be applied to a future referendum or secession process. He also argued that the statements of both the former Premier and the current Premier of Quebec were of little juridical weight. The Attorney General of Canada submitted that it was evident that the Government of Quebec was committed to realizing the secession of Quebec and obtaining for itself and the National Assembly the exclusive power to levy taxes, enact laws, and make treaties— all attributes of a sovereign state.

> No matter what form a unilateral declaration of independence might take in the future, any measure purporting to give to a unilateral declaration the force of law, to the effect that Quebec is no longer a province of Canada, would raise the same basic legal issues as are before the Court in this Reference.[25]

The Attorney General of Canada also emphasized the need for a timely and authoritative opinion on the validity of possible recourse to a U.D.I., noting that the Government of Quebec

> has shown itself to be prepared to do so in circumstances, and within a time frame, that would make it difficult and likely impossible for a

---

[24] A.G. Canada, Reply factum, paras. 27 and 28.

[25] A.G. Canada, Reply factum, para. 29.

case to proceed through the court system to a final decision if the proceedings could only be instituted on the eve, or in the aftermath, of a unilateral declaration of independence.

This issue had developed with particular acuity "in light of the Government of Quebec's refusal to acknowledge the jurisdiction of the courts of Quebec and Canada in relation to the secession process it proposes to follow."[26]

The Supreme Court ruled on the issues relating to justiciability by noting firstly that in a reference, where the Court is acting in an advisory capacity rather than exercising its traditional adjudicative function, the Court may be asked hypothetical questions such as the constitutionality of proposed legislation, and deal with issues that might otherwise not be considered ripe for decision in the context of litigation.[27]

However, even in a reference, the Court should not address "questions that would be inappropriate to answer." In a reference, the focus on whether to answer the question should be on "whether the dispute is appropriately addressed by a court of law." Focusing on criteria enunciated in *Reference Re Canada Assistance Plan (B.C.)*,[28] the Court indicated that the circumstances in which it may decline to answer a reference question as non-justiciable include the following:

1. if to do so would take the Court beyond its own assessment of its proper role in the constitutional framework of our democratic form of government; or

2. if the Court could not give an answer that lies within its area of expertise: the interpretation of law.[29]

With respect to the proper role of the Court, the Reference questions did not "ask the Court to usurp any democratic decision that the people of Quebec may be called upon to make."

> The questions posed by the Governor in Council, as we interpret them, are strictly limited to aspects of the legal framework in which that democratic decision is to be taken.[30]

As regarded the *legal* nature of the questions, in the present Reference "the questions may clearly be interpreted as directed to legal issues, and so interpreted, the Court is in a position to answer them."[31]

---

[26] A.G. Canada, Reply factum, para. 30. Guy Bertrand and his co-counsel in the Reference, Patrick Monahan, had made a similar, telling point; citizens must not be made to face the following dilemma: to be told by the Government of Quebec and the courts that before a U.D.I., their case is too early, and that after a U.D.I., their case is too late.

[27] Para. 25 of the reasons for judgment.

[28] Para. 26 *et seq.* of the reasons for judgment; and [1991] 2 S.C.R. 525, at p. 545.

[29] Para. 26 of the reasons of the Court.

[30] Para. 27.

[31] Para. 28.

In closing its comments on justiciability, the Court added:

> The reference questions raise issues of fundamental public importance. It cannot be said that the questions are too imprecise or ambiguous to permit a proper legal answer. Nor can it be said that the Court has been provided with insufficient information regarding the present context in which the questions arise. Thus, the Court is duty bound in the circumstances to provide its answers.[32]

Question 1: Position of the Attorney General of Canada

The first question, it will be recalled, was formulated as follows:

> Under the Constitution of Canada, can the National Assembly, legislature or government of Quebec effect the secession of Quebec from Canada unilaterally?

The Attorney General of Canada submitted that no institution of the province of Quebec can, under the Constitution of Canada, unilaterally effect the secession of Quebec from Canada.[33] The argument advanced by the Attorney General of Canada was both principled and linear in its approach. It ran along the following broad lines.

Canada is a federal state founded on constitutional government and subject to the rule of law. The Constitution of Canada is the supreme law of Canada. The Courts have a duty to defend and uphold the Constitution, and to ensure that the federal principle is respected. Neither level of government can exceed its constitutional mandate.

The secession of a province from Canada would affect the structure and scope of the Constitution and would have an impact on the federation as a whole. Secession, by its very nature, is extraordinary. It is disruptive, it is destabilizing, it represents a fundamental alteration to the existing constitutional order, and it would terminate the very authority of the Constitution over the seceding territory. In a federal state such as Canada, secession would break the original political commitment to form a union, jeopardizing the network of mutual relationships, obligations, undertakings, and expectations that the decision to unite federally had generated and encouraged.

The Constitution of Canada does not prohibit secession, nor does it expressly permit it. While the Constitution of Canada does not expressly provide for secession, it was the position of the Attorney General of Canada that the Constitution is capable of accommodating *any* alteration to the federation, including such an extraordinary change as the secession of a province.

---

[32] Para. 31.

[33] Factum of the Attorney General of Canada (filed 28 February 1997), paras. 56–119; para. 211.

Secession and the Need for Constitutional Amendment

The powers granted to the provinces and their institutions by the Constitution do not include the power of unilateral secession from the Canadian federation. The secession of a province would necessarily require constitutional amendment. While the Patriation of the Constitution in 1982 altered the means by which constitutional amendments may be effected, it did not alter the fundamental capacity of the Constitution to effect and accommodate change. Such changes have always had to be accomplished through the prevailing constitutional framework.

Since 1982, Part V of the *Constitution Act, 1982*, entitled "Procedure for Amending Constitution of Canada," has contained a comprehensive set of procedures for effecting constitutional change. As the Supreme Court held in the *Quebec Veto Reference,*

> The *Constitution Act, 1982* is now in force. Its legality is neither challenged nor assailable. It contains a new procedure for amending the Constitution which entirely replaces the old one in its legal as well as in its conventional aspects.[34]

Part V of the *Constitution Act, 1982* identifies the institutions and prescribes the requirements for effecting constitutional amendments. Part V sets out five different procedures for constitutional amendment, depending on the subject-matter of the proposed change.

> (1) the general (or "7/50") procedure, which requires the assent of the House of Commons, the Senate (suspensive veto only) and the legislative assemblies of two-thirds of the provinces representing fifty per cent of the population of the provinces: **s. 38** (or s. 42 for the matters listed therein);

> (2) the unanimity procedure, which requires the assent of the House of Commons, the Senate (suspensive veto only) and the legislative assemblies of all of the provinces: **s. 41**;

> (3) the "one or more but not all provinces" (including the "bilateral") procedure, which requires the assent of the House of Commons, the Senate (suspensive veto only) and of the legislative assembly of the province(s) to which the amendment applies: **s. 43**;

> (4) the federal unilateral procedure, permitting amendment by Act of Parliament alone: **s. 44**;

> (5) the provincial unilateral procedure, permitting amendment by an Act of a provincial legislature alone: **s. 45**.

It is clear that the constitutional amendment or amendments necessary to effect the secession of a province from Canada cannot be brought within the terms of the unilateral provincial amending procedure set out in s. 45 of the *Constitution Act, 1982*. Section 45 allows for unilateral amendments

---

[34] Factum of the Attorney General of Canada, para. 91. The citation is *Reference re Objection to a Resolution to Amend the Constitution*, [1982] 2 S.C.R. 793, at p. 806.

only in limited circumstances; such amendments must relate to the "constitution of the province," i.e., to matters internal to the province and its institutions. The secession of a province, with its profound alteration to Canada's constitutional order and its impact on the federal principle, would clearly lie beyond the authority of a province to effect unilaterally under s. 45.[35]

This is demonstrated by the three key powers the Government of Quebec has consistently identified as the attributes of sovereignty: the *exclusive* power to enact all laws, to levy all taxes, and to conclude all treaties applying to Quebec. The exclusive exercise of these powers—contemplated both by the Government of Quebec's Draft Bill, *An Act respecting the sovereignty of Québec*, and Bill 1, *An Act respecting the future of Québec*, would clearly lie outside the competence of a province under the Constitution of Canada. It would require more than a mere amendment to the internal constitution of the province to remove these powers from the jurisdiction of the Parliament of Canada and the federal executive.

In summary, the position of the Attorney General of Canada was that secession would necessarily require constitutional amendment, and that unilateral secession would be beyond the power of a province under s. 45 of the *Constitution Act, 1982*. While the National Assembly of Quebec would be a necessary participant in such a constitutional amendment process, other Part V institutional participants beyond those of the province of Quebec alone would also have a role. Section 45 of the *Constitution Act, 1982* having been ruled out as a means for effecting the unilateral secession of a province, the Attorney General of Canada submitted that it was unnecessary to address other issues in order to answer the first Reference question; in particular, the Court need not consider arguments as to which of the amending procedures under the Constitution of Canada or what other constitutional principles might apply in the event of a potential secession.[36]

In conclusion, the Reference, in the view of the Attorney General of Canada, "is about whether the institutions of Quebec have the power to effect the secession of that province *unilaterally* under Canadian constitutional law and whether they have a right to do so under international law."[37]

> The unilateral secession of a province from Canada would run counter to this country's tradition of constitutional government, to its regard for the rule of law and its respect for the rights of citizens, to the duty of Canadian courts to defend the Constitution, and to the federal principle which the Constitution enshrines.[38]

---

[35] This argument is developed in more detail in the factum of the Attorney General of Canada, in paras. 99–115, with reference notably to *O.P.S.E.U. v. Ontario (A.G.)*, [1987] 2 S.C.R. 2.

[36] Factum of the A.G. Canada, paras. 114–116. This position is further articulated in paras. 40–47 ("The Scope of the Questions") of the Reply factum of the A.G. Canada, and in paras. 41–43 of the Written Response of the A.G. Canada to Questions from the Supreme Court.

[37] Reply factum, A.G. Canada, para. 47.

[38] Factum, A.G. Canada, para. 75.

Question 1: Opinion of the Supreme Court

The Court's approach was also a principled one, but less linear, and in some ways on a higher plane, as befitted the advisory role of the Court. The Court began by emphasizing that the *Constitution Act, 1982* is in force and its legality is unassailable. The Constitution of Canada includes the constitutional texts enumerated in s. 52(2) of the *Constitution Act, 1982*, which "have a primary place in determining constitutional rules," as well as the global system of "supporting principles and rules" that "emerge from an understanding of the constitutional text itself, the historical context, and previous judicial interpretations of constitutional meaning." In the view of the Court,

> There are four fundamental and organizing principles of the Constitution which are relevant to addressing the question before us (although this enumeration is by no means exhaustive): federalism; democracy; constitutionalism and the rule of law; and respect for minorities.[39]

The Court devoted several pages of its opinion to providing a sensitive and thoughtful outline of the history and significance of Canadian Confederation, emphasizing that "[i]n our constitutional tradition, legality and legitimacy are linked," and that "our constitutional history demonstrates that our governing institutions have adapted and changed to reflect changing social and political values." This has, the Court added, "generally been accomplished by methods that have ensured continuity, stability and legal order."[40] The historical review underscored the fact that

> the evolution of our constitutional arrangements has been characterized by adherence to the rule of law, respect for democratic institutions, the accommodation of minorities; insistence that governments adhere to constitutional conduct and a desire for continuity and stability.[41]

Constitutional Principles

The Court then turned to an analysis of the nature and scope of the underlying principles relevant to the *Secession Reference*. The *Provincial Judges Reference*[42] had recently confirmed that such principles, long recognized in the Court's previous jurisprudence, may be used for two purposes: "to fill out gaps in the express terms of the constitutional scheme," and to construe the provisions of the written Constitution. There was no suggestion, however, in the *Provincial Judges Reference* that unwritten constitutional principles can be employed to supersede the terms of the written Constitution. To the contrary, as the Chief Justice noted: "There are many important reasons for the preference of a written constitution over an unwritten one, not the least of which is the promotion of legal certainty and through it the legitimacy of judicial review."[43]

---

[39] *Quebec Secession Reference, supra*, reasons for judgment, para. 32.

[40] *Id.*, para. 33 *et seq.*

[41] Para. 48.

[42] [1997] 3 S.C.R. 3, at p. 69, para. 95.

[43] *Id.*, at p. 68, para. 93.

The Supreme Court came back to this point in the *Quebec Secession Reference*, stating:

> In the *Provincial Judges Reference* [...], we cautioned that the recognition of these constitutional principles [...] could not be taken as an invitation to dispense with the written text of the Constitution. On the contrary, we confirmed that there are compelling reasons to insist upon the primacy of our written constitution. A written constitution promotes legal certainty and predictability, and it provides a foundation and a touchstone for the exercise of constitutional judicial review.[44]

That said, the Court went on to note that in certain circumstances, underlying constitutional principles may give rise to substantive legal obligations, which may in turn be "very abstract and general" or "more precise and specific" in character. "The principles are not merely descriptive, but are also invested with a powerful normative force and are binding upon both courts and governments."

Federalism and Democracy

The Court first examined the principle of *federalism*, which, it said, "recognizes the diversity of the component parts of Confederation," "facilitates democratic participation," and "facilitates the pursuit of collective goals by cultural and linguistic minorities which form the majority within a particular province."[45] The Court acknowledged and affirmed Quebec's distinctiveness in this context.

> This is the case in Quebec, where the majority of the population is French-speaking, and which possesses a distinct culture. This is not merely the result of chance. The social and demographic reality of Quebec explains the existence of the province of Quebec as a political unit and indeed, was one of the essential reasons for establishing a federal structure for the Canadian union in 1867. [...] The federal structure adopted at Confederation enabled French-speaking Canadians to form a numerical majority in the province of Quebec, and so exercise the considerable provincial power conferred by the *Constitution Act, 1867* in such a way as to promote their language and culture. It also made provision for certain guaranteed representation within the federal Parliament itself.[46]

Turning next to the principle of *democracy*, "a fundamental value in our constitutional law and political culture," the Court underlined that while democracy is "commonly understood as being a political system of majority rule," it is not only concerned with process but with substance; with the accommodation of cultural and group identities, the promotion of self-government, the pursuit of social justice and equality, and enhanced participation of individuals and groups in society, to mention some of the goals and values inherent in the principle.[47]

---

[44] *Reference re Secession of Quebec, supra*, para. 53.

[45] *Id.*, paras. 58 and 59.

[46] *Id.*, para. 59.

[47] Paras. 63 and 64.

The Court noted that the relationship between democracy and federalism in Canada means that "there may be different and equally legitimate majorities" at the provincial or territorial and federal levels.

> A federal system of government enables different provinces to pursue policies responsive to the particular concerns and interests of people in that province. At the same time, Canada as a whole is also a democratic community in which citizens construct and achieve goals on a national scale through a federal government acting within the limits of its jurisdiction. The function of federalism is to enable citizens to participate concurrently in different collectivities and to pursue goals at both a provincial and federal level.[48]

Democracy and the Rule of Law

The Court also insisted upon the essential interaction between the principles of democracy and the rule of law.

> [D]emocracy in any real sense of the word cannot exist without the rule of law. It is the law that creates the framework within which the "sovereign will" is to be ascertained and implemented. To be accorded legitimacy, democratic institutions must rest, ultimately, on a legal foundation.

At the same time, "a system of government cannot survive through adherence to the law alone."

> A political system must also possess legitimacy, and in our political culture, that requires an interaction between the rule of law and the democratic principle. The system must be capable of reflecting the aspirations of the people.

But there is more to this interaction, the Court hastened to add.

> Our law's claim to legitimacy also rests on an appeal to moral values, many of which are embedded in our constitutional structure. It would be a grave mistake to equate legitimacy with the "sovereign will" or majority rule alone, to the exclusion of other constitutional values.[49]

The Court underscored the fact that a healthy democracy "requires a continuous process of discussion." Dogmatic, doctrinaire, and absolutist approaches to complex public policy issues have little place in modern, representative, and inclusivist government.

> At both the federal and provincial level, by its very nature, the need to build majorities necessitates compromise, negotiation, and deliberation. No one has a monopoly on truth, and our system is predicated on the faith that in the marketplace of ideas, the best solutions to public problems will rise to the top. Inevitably, there will be dissenting voices. A democratic system of government is committed to considering those

---

[48] Para. 66.

[49] Para. 67. This stricture would have to be borne in mind when equating democracy with "the supremacy of the sovereign will of the people, in this case potentially to be expressed by Quebecers in support of unilateral secession." (Para. 61.)

dissenting voices, and seeking to acknowledge and address those voices in the laws by which all in the community must live.[50]

In a remarkable fashion, the Court then linked the democratic principle to the formal process of constitutional amendment set out in Part V of the *Constitution Act, 1982*. By virtue of s. 46(1), amendment procedures may be initiated by the Senate, the House of Commons, or the legislative assembly of any province.[51] The Court characterized this power (or capacity) as "a right to initiate constitutional change" that had been conferred, by the *Constitution Act, 1982*, "on each participant in Confederation."

> In our view, the existence of this right imposes a corresponding duty on the participants in Confederation to engage in constitutional discussions in order to acknowledge and address democratic expressions of a desire for change in other provinces. This duty is inherent in the democratic principle which is a fundamental predicate of our system of governance.[52]

Constitutionalism and the Rule of Law

The Court's analysis next turned to the principles of *constitutionalism* and the *rule of law*. "At its most basic level, the rule of law vouchsafes to the citizens and residents of the country a stable, predictable, ordered society in which to conduct their affairs."[53] Drawing on the *Manitoba Language Rights Reference* and the *Provincial Judges Reference*, the Court outlined the three aspects of the rule of law as being, first, that the law is supreme over the acts of both government and the governed ("There is, in short, one law for all"); second, that a system of positive laws, embodying the concept of a normative order, must be maintained; and third, that the exercise of public power must find its source in legal rules.[54]

The constitutionalism principle is similar, but not identical, to the rule of law principle, the Court explained.

> The essence of constitutionalism in Canada is embodied in s. 52(1) of the *Constitution Act, 1982*, which provides that "[t]he Constitution of Canada is the supreme law of Canada, and any law that is inconsistent with the provisions of the Constitution is, to the extent of the inconsistency, of no force or effect." Simply put, the constitutionalism principle requires that all governmental action comply with the Constitution. The rule of law principle requires that all governmental action must comply with the law, including the Constitution.[55]

---

[50] Para. 68.

[51] This point was emphasized in the factum filed on behalf of Singh *et al.*: "It is possible, by lawful means under Part V, to accomplish *any* conceivable constitutional change, *including* the independence of Quebec, which might be decided on by the country. [...] *It is open to the National Assembly of Quebec, under s. 46(1), to initiate any such amendment at anytime.*" (Singh factum, para. 12; emphasis in original.)

[52] Para. 69.

[53] Para. 70.

[54] Para. 71.

[55] Para. 72.

The Court underlined that the Constitution "binds all governments, both federal and provincial."

> They may not transgress its provisions: indeed, their sole claim to exercise lawful authority rests in the powers allocated to them under the Constitution, and can come from no other source.[56]

Constitutionalism and Democracy

In this context, the Court illustrated the "scope and importance" of the principles of the rule of law and constitutionalism by considering "why a constitution is entrenched beyond the reach of simple majority rule":

> First, a constitution may provide an added safeguard for fundamental human rights and individual freedoms which might otherwise be susceptible to government interference. [...] Second, a constitution may seek to ensure that vulnerable minority groups are endowed with the institutions and rights necessary to maintain and promote their identities against the assimilative pressures of the majority. And third, a constitution may provide for a division of political power that allocates political power amongst different levels of government.

That latter purpose, the Court added, in a comment that recalled to mind particularly the Draft Bill and Bill 1, would be negated if one democratically elected level of government "could usurp the powers of the other simply by exercising legislative power to allocate additional political power to itself unilaterally."[57]

The argument, the Court went on to state, that the Constitution "may be legitimately circumvented by resort to a majority vote in a province-wide referendum" is one that is "superficially persuasive" given its appeal to principles such as democracy and self-government.

> In short, it is suggested that as the notion of popular sovereignty underlies the legitimacy of our existing constitutional arrangements, so the same popular sovereignty that originally led to the present Constitution must (it is argued) also permit "the people" in their exercise of popular sovereignty to secede by majority vote alone.[58]

That argument is erroneous, the Court ruled, "because it misunderstands the meaning of popular sovereignty and the essence of a constitutional democracy."

> Canadians have never accepted that ours is a system of simple majority rule. Our principle of democracy, taken in conjunction with the other constitutional principles discussed here, is richer.[59]

In a democracy predicated on constitutional government, constitutional rules are binding, "not in the sense of frustrating the will of a majority of

---

[56] *Ibid.*

[57] Paras. 73 and 74.

[58] Para. 75.

[59] Para. 76.

a province, but as defining the majority which must be consulted in order to alter the fundamental balances of political power (including the spheres of autonomy guaranteed by the principle of federalism), individual rights, and minority rights in our society." Of course, the Court acknowledged,

> those constitutional rules are themselves amenable to amendment, but only through a process of negotiation which ensures that there is an opportunity for the constitutionally defined rights of all the parties to be respected and reconciled.[60]

In this fashion, the Court emphasized, "our belief in democracy may be harmonized with our belief in constitutionalism." Again, the Court returned to the formal requirements of the procedure for amending the Constitution itself to underscore its point.

> Constitutional amendment often requires some form of substantial consensus precisely because the content of the underlying principles of our Constitution demand it. By requiring broad support in the form of an "enhanced majority" to achieve constitutional change, the Constitution ensures that minority interests must be addressed before proposed changes which would affect them may be enacted.[61]

Constitutionalism is not incompatible with democratic government. Constitutionalism makes a democratic system possible "by creating an orderly framework within which people may make political decisions."

> Viewed correctly, constitutionalism and the rule of law are not in conflict with democracy; rather, they are essential to it.[62]

The Protection of Minorities

Finally, the Court reviewed the fourth principle relevant to the secession issue, the *protection of minorities*. The Court noted that long before the advent of the *Canadian Charter of Rights and Freedoms* in 1982, there existed a number of entrenched constitutional provisions protecting minority language, religion, and education rights, and highlighted the fact that even though those guarantees were the product of historical compromises, "that does not render them unprincipled." The Court emphasized that the protection of minority rights is itself "an independent principle underlying our constitutional order," and one "clearly reflected in the *Charter*'s provisions for the protection of minority rights."[63]

Consistent with the historical tradition of respect for minorities in Canada was the inclusion, in the *Constitution Act, 1982*, of express protections for existing aboriginal and treaty rights (s. 35) and a non-derogation provision (s. 25) respecting the rights of aboriginal peoples.

---

[60] *Ibid.*

[61] Para. 77.

[62] Para. 78.

[63] Paras. 79 and 80.

The protection of these rights, so recently and arduously achieved, whether looked at in their own right or as part of the larger concern with minorities, reflects an important underlying constitutional value.[64]

Constitutional Principles in the Secession Context

"Secession," the Court underlined, in applying the constitutional principles to Question 1 of the Reference, "is a legal act as much as a political one." By Question 1, "we are asked to rule on the legality of unilateral secession" under the Constitution of Canada. This, the Court held, was an "appropriate question," because "the legality of unilateral secession must be evaluated, at least in the first instance, from the perspective of the domestic legal order of the state from which the unit seeks to withdraw."[65]

The Attorney General of Canada had argued in the factum filed in the Reference that unilateral secession was illegal under the Constitution of Canada, and that for secession to be effected lawfully, the Constitution would need to be amended. This view was shared by most, if not all, legal scholars who had written on this issue. However, between the time of the filing of the federal factum in February 1997 and the hearing of the Reference in February 1998, several commentators had put into doubt the application of the Part V amending procedures of the *Constitution Act, 1982* to the secession of a province. Professor MacLauchlan contended that Part V assumes the ongoing existence of Canada and was never intended to apply to secession.[66] Professors Howse and Malkin argued that the Part V amending procedures "cannot be used so as to confer constitutionality on the act of secession itself."[67] Professor Frémont and his co-author, Mr. Boudreault, took these arguments one step further and contended that the secession of Quebec is constitutionally impossible because the Constitution would be the instrument of its own destruction.

> [D]es principes supra constitutionnels feraient que l'ordre constitutionnel canadien serait tout simplement incapable d'ingérer la sécession du Québec. Il serait alors lui-même condamné à procéder à sa propre révolution.[68]

Therefore, they concluded, the only way to accomplish secession would be through a revolution in the legal order.

The Attorney General of Canada categorically rejected and rebutted these arguments in the written response to questions from the Court filed on March 6, 1998.[69] The Attorney General of Canada fundamentally disagreed

---

[64] Para. 82.

[65] Para. 83.

[66] H. Wade MacLauchlan, "Accounting for Democracy and the Rule of Law in the Quebec Secession Reference" (1997) 76 Can. Bar. Rev. 155.

[67] Robert Howse and Alissa Malkin, "Canadians Are a Sovereign People: How the Supreme Court Should Approach the Reference on Quebec Secession" (1997) 76 Can. Bar. Rev. 186.

[68] Jacques Frémont and François Boudreault, "Supraconstitutionnalité canadienne et sécession du Québec" (1997) 8 N.J.C.L. 163 at p. 203.

[69] Written Response of the Attorney General of Canada to Questions from the Supreme Court of Canada (6 March 1998), paras. 25–30. For a solid refutation of many of the arguments

with all assertions to the effect that unwritten constitutional principles precluded the secession of a province by way of constitutional amendment.

Secession Requires a Constitutional Amendment

The Supreme Court of Canada also dismissed these arguments in its opinion in the *Quebec Secession Reference*, and held that, legally, secession would require a constitutional amendment.

> *The secession of a province from Canada must be considered, in legal terms, to require an amendment to the Constitution,* which perforce requires negotiation. The amendments necessary to achieve a secession could be radical and extensive. Some commentators have suggested that secession could be a change of such a magnitude that it could not be considered to be merely an amendment to the Constitution. We are not persuaded by this contention. It is of course true that the Constitution is silent as to the ability of a province to secede from Confederation but, although the Constitution neither expressly authorizes nor prohibits secession, an act of secession would purport to alter the governance of Canadian territory in a manner which undoubtedly is inconsistent with our current constitutional arrangements. *The fact that those changes would be profound,* or that they would purport to have a significance with respect to international law, *does not negate their nature as amendments to the Constitution of Canada.*

> The Constitution is the expression of the sovereignty of the people of Canada. It lies within the power of the people of Canada, acting through their various governments duly elected and recognized under the Constitution, to effect whatever constitutional arrangements are desired within Canadian territory, including, should it be so desired, the secession of Quebec from Canada.[70]

The Court then focused on the wording of Question 1 of the Reference and whether it would be constitutional (assuming the existence of a political will to do so) for the National Assembly, legislature, or Government of Quebec to effect the secession of Quebec from Canada *unilaterally*. In one sense, the Court noted, "any step towards a constitutional amendment initiated by a single actor on the constitutional stage" is "unilateral," but this was not the meaning intended in the first Question.

> Rather, what is claimed by a right to secede "unilaterally" is the right to effectuate secession without prior negotiations *with the other provinces and the federal government.* At issue is not the legality of the first step but *the legality of the final act of purported unilateral secession.*[71]

The Court went on to examine the "supposed juridical basis" for an act of unilateral secession; i.e., "a clear expression of democratic will in a

---

that had been previously put forward in an attempt to escape the application of the amendment procedures set out in the *Constitution Act, 1982* to secession, see Jeremy Webber, "The Legality of a Unilateral Declaration of Independence Under Canadian Law" (1997) 42 McGill L.J. 281.

[70] *Reference re Secession of Quebec, supra,* paras. 84 and 85; emphasis added.

[71] *Id.,* para. 86; emphasis added.

referendum in the province of Quebec." The Court mentioned that the Constitution "does not itself address the use of a referendum procedure, and the results of a referendum have no direct role or legal effect in our constitutional scheme," although there is no doubt that a referendum "may provide a democratic method of ascertaining the views of the electorate on important political questions." The democratic principle would require that "considerable weight be given to a clear expression by the people of Quebec of their will to secede from Canada, even though a referendum, in itself and without more, has no direct legal effect, and could not in itself bring about unilateral secession."

> [A]n expression of the democratic will of the people of the province carries weight, in that it would *confer legitimacy on the efforts* of the government of Quebec *to initiate the Constitution's amendment process* in order to secede by constitutional means.[72]

The Court now returned to its earlier equation, which had been posited in general terms,[73] that the *Constitution Act, 1982,* by conferring a right on each participant in Confederation to initiate constitutional change, imposes a corresponding duty on all the participants to engage in constitutional discussions.

> *The amendment of the Constitution begins with a political process undertaken pursuant to the Constitution itself.* In Canada, the initiative for constitutional amendment is the responsibility of democratically elected representatives of the participants in Confederation. Those representatives may, of course, take their cue from a referendum, but *in legal terms, constitution-making in Canada, as in many countries, is undertaken by the democratically elected representatives of the people.*[74]

A Reciprocal Duty to Negotiate

Having regard to the federalism principle and the democratic principle, the "clear repudiation of the existing constitutional order" and the "clear expression of a desire to pursue secession by the population of the province" would, in the context of the constitutional amendment procedures, create "a reciprocal obligation on all parties to Confederation to negotiate changes to respond to that desire."

> The corollary of a legitimate attempt by one participant in Confederation to seek an amendment to the Constitution is an obligation on all parties to come to the negotiating table. The clear repudiation by the people of Quebec of the existing contitutional order would confer legitimacy on demands for secession, and place an obligation on the other provinces

---

[72] Paras. 86 and 87; emphasis added. The Court went on to note: "In this context, we refer to a 'clear' majority as a qualitative evaluation. The referendum result, if it is to be taken as an expression of the democratic will, must be free of ambiguity both in terms of the question asked and in terms of the support it achieves."

[73] Para. 69, discussed *supra.* See Part V, *Constitution Act, 1982,* "Procedure for Amending Constitution of Canada."

[74] Para. 88; emphasis added.

and the federal government to acknowledge and respect that expression of democratic will by entering into negotiations and conducting them in accordance with the underlying constitutional principles already discussed.[75]

Thus, the obligation to negotiate would arise after a clear expression of a desire to pursue secession. It would be a reciprocal obligation on all parties to negotiate in accordance with the principles of federalism, democracy, constitutionalism and the rule of law, and the protection of minorities. The conduct of the parties, the Court added, would be governed by the same constitutional principles. The obligation to negotiate on the basis of those principles led the Court to reject two extreme "absolutist propositions". The first was that there would be a legal obligation on the federal government and the other provinces to agree to the secession of a province, "subject only to negotiation of the logistical details of secession." This proposition—"attributed either to the supposed implications of the democratic principle of the Constitution, or to the international law principle of self-determination of peoples"—was firmly rejected by the Court.

> [W]e cannot accept this view. We hold that Quebec could not purport to invoke a right of self-determination such as to dictate the terms of the proposed secession to the other parties: *that would not be a negotiation at all.* As well, it would be naive to expect that the substantive goal of secession could readily be distinguished from the practical details of secession. The devil would be in the details. The democracy principle, as we have emphasized, cannot be invoked to trump the principles of federalism and rule of law, the rights of individuals and minorities, or the operation of democracy in the other provinces or in Canada as a whole. *No negotiations could be effective if their ultimate outcome, secession, is cast as an absolute legal entitlement* based upon an obligation *to give effect to that act of secession in the Constitution.* Such a foregone conclusion would actually undermine the obligation to negotiate and render it hollow.[76]

"However," the Court continued, "we are equally unable to accept the reverse proposition, that a clear expression of self-determination by the people of Quebec would impose <u>no</u> obligations upon the other provinces or the federal government."

> The *continued existence and operation of the Canadian constitutional order cannot remain indifferent to clear expression of a clear majority of Quebecers that they no longer wish to remain in Canada.* This would amount to the assertion that other constitutionally recognized principles necessarily trump the clearly expressed democratic will of the people of Quebec. Such a proposition fails to give sufficient weight to the *underlying constitutional principles that must inform the amendment process,* including the principles of democracy and federalism. The rights of other provinces and the federal government cannot deny the right of the government of Quebec to pursue secession, should a clear majority of the people of Quebec choose that goal, *so long as in*

---

[75] *Ibid.*

[76] Paras. 90 and 91; emphasis added.

doing so, Quebec respects the rights of others. Negotiations would be necessary to address the interests of the federal government, of Quebec and the other provinces, and other participants, as well as the rights of all Canadians both within and outside Quebec.[77]

The rejection of both extremes of the spectrum—at the one end, an absolute legal entitlement and obligation to achieve secession, and at the other end, no obligation whatsoever to address a clear desire to pursue secession—put the focus on reasonableness and good faith in negotiations that would themselves have to be conducted within a framework of constitutional principles.

> The negotiation process precipitated by a decision of the clear majority of the population of Quebec on a clear question to pursue secession would require the reconciliation of various rights and obligations by the representatives of two legitimate majorities, namely the clear majority of the population of Quebec, and the clear majority of Canada as a whole, whatever that may be. There can be no suggestion that either of these majorities "trumps" the other. A political majority that does not act in accordance with the underlying constitutional principles we have identified puts at risk the legitimacy of the exercise of its rights.[78]

The Court cautioned against the kind of intransigence in the assertion of rights, to the exclusion of other values, that could put in jeopardy the dynamics of a positive negotiation process, with regard to the larger consequences attendant upon failure—not to achieve a particular result, *per se*, but rather, to comport oneself in the negotiations in a manner that would have attempted to respect and to reconcile, to the extent reasonably possible, the rights and interests of all.

> In such circumstances, the conduct of the parties assumes primary constitutional significance. The negotiation process must be conducted with an eye to the constitutional principles we have outlined, which must inform the actions of all the participants in the negotiation process.
>
> Refusal of a party to conduct negotiations in a manner consistent with constitutional principles and values would seriously put at risk the legitimacy of that party's assertion of its rights, and perhaps the negotiation process as a whole. Those who quite legitimately insist upon the importance of upholding the rule of law cannot at the same time be oblivious to the need to act in conformity with constitutional principles and values, and so do their part to contribute to the maintenance and promotion of an environment in which the rule of law may flourish.[79]

Having said that, the Court was quick to recognize that even negotiations conducted in the utmost good faith could be fraught with difficulty.

> No one can predict the course that such negotiations might take. The possibility that they might not lead to an agreement amongst the parties

---

[77] Para. 92; Court's underlining; emphasis in italics, added.

[78] Para. 93.

[79] Paras. 94 and 95.

must be recognized. Negotiations following a referendum vote in favour of secession would inevitably address a wide range of issues, many of great import. After 131 years of Confederation, there exists, inevitably, a high level of integration in economic, political and social institutions across Canada.[80]

The Court noted that there is "a national economy and national debt"; "boundary issues"; "linguistic and cultural minorities, including aboriginal peoples, unevenly distributed across the country who look to the Constitution of Canada for protection of their rights."

> Of course, secession would give rise to many issues of great complexity and difficulty. *These would have to be resolved within the overall framework of the rule of law*, thereby assuring Canadians resident in Quebec and elsewhere a measure of stability in what would likely be a period of considerable upheaval and uncertainty. Nobody seriously suggests that our national existence, seamless in so many aspects, could be effortlessly separated along what are now the provincial boundaries of Quebec.[81]

Negotiations "would undoubtedly be difficult" the Court stated. The Court refrained from any conjecture about what might happen in the event of an impasse, repeating simply that under the Constitution, an amendment would have to be negotiated to effect secession.

> While the negotiators would have to contemplate the possibility of secession, there would be no absolute legal entitlement to it and no assumption that an agreement reconciling all relevant rights and obligations would actually be reached. It is foreseeable that even negotiations carried out in conformity with the underlying constitutional principles could reach an impasse. We need not speculate here as to what would then transpire. Under the Constitution, secession requires that an amendment be negotiated.[82]

This was entirely consonant with the position taken by the Attorney General of Canada, who had argued strenuously, through counsel, that the Court need not and should not be drawn into speculation about hypotheses and scenarios of impasse, or about what remedial or savings doctrines might be invoked by a court *in extremis*. To the extent, for example, that something less than full compliance with the constitutional amendment procedure might, in some extreme situation of manifest and persistent political deadlock, be contemplated by the courts at some point, this could only be in circumstances of demonstrable exigency, and then, in furtherance of the Constitution's underlying principles—the first imperative being to protect the rule of law and preserve the Constitution's basic values.[83]

---

[80] Para. 96.

[81] *Ibid.*; emphasis added.

[82] Para. 97.

[83] See Written Response of the A.G. Canada to Questions from the Supreme Court of Canada (6 March 1998), paras. 37–43. The Attorney General of Canada added (para. 44): "It must be emphasized that the risks of political impasse, with its attendant consequences, are

Role of the Courts and the Political Actors

The Court devoted several paragraphs of its opinion to distinguishing between the "respective roles of the courts and the political actors in discharging the constitutional obligations" identified by the Court in the Reference. The Court recalled that in the *Patriation Reference*, a distinction was made between "the law of the Constitution, which, generally speaking, will be enforced by the Courts, and other constitutional rules, such as the conventions of the Constitution, which carry only political sanctions." The Court went on to emphasize that "judicial intervention, even in relation to the <u>law</u> of the Constitution, is subject to the Court's appreciation of its proper role in the constitutional scheme."[84]

The role of the Court in the Reference "is limited to the identification of the relevant aspects of the Constitution in their broadest sense."

> We have interpreted the questions as relating *to the constitutional framework within which political decisions may ultimately be made.* Within that framework, the workings of the political process are complex and can only be resolved by means of political judgments and evaluations. *The Court has no supervisory role over the political aspects of constitutional negotiations.*[85]

Matters such as what constitutes "a clear majority on a clear question in favour of secession," thereby triggering negotiations, were matters for political, not judicial, evaluation. While a right and a duty to negotiate secession "cannot be built on an alleged expression of democratic will if the expression of democratic will is itself fraught with ambiguities," only the political actors would be in a position to resolve those ambiguities one way or another. Similarly, if the duty to negotiate was in fact triggered, the distinction between the legitimate defence of interests and the taking of intransigent positions ignoring the interests of others would also be a matter that "defies legal analysis".[86]

> The Court would not have access to all of the information available to the political actors, and *the methods appropriate for the search for truth in a court of law are ill-suited to getting to the bottom of constitutional negotiations.* To the extent that the questions are political in nature, it is not the role of the judiciary to interpose its own views on the different negotiating positions of the parties, even if it were invited to do so. Rather, *it is the obligation of the elected representatives to give concrete form to the discharge of their constitutional obligations which only they and their electors can ultimately assess.* The reconciliation of the various legitimate constitutional interests outlined above is necessarily

---

far greater if one is operating outside the framework of the rule of law and the Constitution than under it."

[84] *Reference re Secession of Quebec, supra,* para. 98; underlining in original. The first proposition is trite law; the second appears to be somewhat novel on its face, but the Court goes on to link it to the issue of justiciability and judicial restraint (para. 99).

[85] Para. 100.

[86] Paras. 100 and 101.

committed to the political rather than the judicial realm, precisely
because that reconciliation can only be achieved through the give and
take of the negotiation process. *Having established the legal framework*, it would be for the democratically elected leadership of the
various participants to resolve their differences.[87]

The Court stressed that the non-justiciability of "political issues that
lack a legal component" does not mean that the "surrounding constitutional
framework" loses its "binding status," or that constitutional duties could be
breached "without incurring serious legal repercussions".

Where there are legal rights there are remedies, but [...] the appropriate
recourse in some circumstances lies through the workings of the
political process rather than the courts.[88]

Interestingly, the Court adverted to the "important ramifications at the
international level" that a breach in the constitutional duty to negotiate in
accordance with the four constitutional principles outlined by the Court
would engender.

[A] *failure* of the duty to *undertake negotiations and pursue them
according to constitutional principles may undermine that government's
claim to legitimacy* which is generally a precondition for recognition
by the international community. *Conversely*, violations of those principles
by the federal or other provincial governments responding to the request
for secession *may undermine their legitimacy*. Thus, *a Quebec that
had negotiated in conformity with constitutional principles and values*
in the face of *unreasonable intransigence* on the part of other participants
at the federal or provincial level *would be more likely to be recognized
than a Quebec which did not itself act according to constitutional*

---

[87] Para. 101; emphasis added. This is consistent with the position advanced by the Attorney
General of Canada: "[56] It is, in part, because the rights of all Canadian citizens, including
minorities and aboriginal peoples, stand to be affected by secession that the Government of
Canada is seeking confirmation by the Court in this Reference that the Canadian constitutional framework applies to a secessionist claim and that *unilateral* secession is illegal under
the Constitution. Such confirmation will secure a framework that will allow the Government
of Canada to be in a better position to take into account the rights of affected citizens and
groups. [57] Of course, Canadians are not only represented by the Government of Canada
but by Parliament and the provincial legislatures. Both the houses of Parliament and the
provincial legislative assemblies have a role to play under the constitutional amendment
procedures set out in Part V of the *Constitution Act, 1982*. In exercising that role, each
relevant institution must make a political judgment about its mandate to authorize the proposed amendment. [59] In sum, there is no doubt that as a matter of basic principle, the
Government of Canada has a general and continuing duty, as do other governments, to
respect the Constitution and the rule of law, notably with respect to any secession process. In
complying with this duty, however, it is both the prerogative and the responsibility of the
Government of Canada to assess the prevailing public environment and examine the range of
legal and policy options open to it, and to exercise its best judgment in determining what
particular course of conduct to pursue in responding to the exigencies of the situation. At all
times, the Government of Canada will be guided by the interests of Canadian citizens and by
the fundamental principle of the rule of law, which is at the heart of our constitutional and
democratic system." Written Response of A.G. Canada to Questions from the Supreme Court
(6 March 1998).

[88] Para. 102.

principles in the negotiation process. Both the *legality* of the acts of the parties to the negotiation process *under Canadian law*, and *the perceived legitimacy* of such action, would be important considerations in the recognition process. *In this way*, the adherence of the parties *to the obligation to negotiate* would be *evaluated* in an indirect manner on the international plane.[89]

By emphasizing the eventual role of the international community in the process of recognizing a new, independent state, and in suggesting considerations related to both legality and legitimacy by which the actions of the political actors in Canada and Quebec may be weighed in the balance as to whether to grant or to withhold recognition, the Court has fashioned a powerful practical incentive for all parties to any process aimed at effecting the secession of Quebec from Canada to conduct the negotiations within the constitutional framework of federalism, democracy, constitutionalism itself and the rule of law, as well as the protection of minorities.

In answering Question 1, then, the Court stated that *unilateral secession* (i.e., without negotiations within the constitutional framework) *cannot* be accomplished by the National Assembly, the legislature, or government of Quebec and be considered "a lawful act".

> Any attempt to effect the secession of a province from Canada must be undertaken pursuant to the Constitution of Canada, or else violate the Canadian legal order.[90]

At the same time, the existence and operation of the Canadian constitutional order "cannot remain unaffected by the unambiguous expression of a clear majority of Quebecers that they no longer wish to remain in Canada." If secession negotiations were undertaken, both Canada's Constitution and the country's history would require the parties to try to reconcile the interests of all Canadians "within a framework that emphasizes constitutional responsibilities as much as it does constitutional rights."[91]

What Amendment Procedure Would Apply

During the course of the Reference, a number of the interveners had urged the Court to examine which of the Part V constitutional amending procedures would apply to effect the secession of Quebec from Canada.[92]

---

[89] Para. 103.

[90] Para. 104.

[91] *Ibid.*

[92] Of these interveners, all agreed with the position of the Attorney General of Canada that the unilateral provincial procedure (s. 45 of the *Constitution Act, 1982*) would not apply, but several argued that the Court could or should go further in its analysis. The Attorney General of Saskatchewan submitted that the "one or more but not all provinces" procedure (s. 43) was also ruled out, and that either unanimity (s. 41) or the general amending procedure (seven provinces representing 50% of the population: s. 38) would apply, although it would be "too speculative" in this Reference to attempt to determine which one of the two was the correct procedure. The Attorney General of Manitoba also cast some doubt on the s. 43 procedure, while the Minister of Justice for the Government of the Yukon argued that it was

The Attorney General of Canada consistently took the position that the first Reference question was addressed only to whether the institutions of the province of Quebec could, under the Constitution of Canada, *unilaterally* effect the secession of Quebec, and that once this question was answered in the negative, there would be no need to go beyond the issue of unilateralism and to consider arguments as to which of the amending procedures under the Constitution might apply in the event of a potential secession. Question 1 did not ask *how* the secession of Quebec could be effected under the Constitution.[93]

This position appeared to find favour with the Court, which stated:

> It will be noted that *Question 1 does not ask how secession could be achieved in a constitutional manner*, but addresses one form of secession only, namely *unilateral* secession. Although the applicability of various procedures to achieve lawful secession was raised in argument, each option would require us to assume the existence of facts that at this stage are unknown. In accordance with the usual rule of prudence in constitutional cases, *we refrain from pronouncing on the applicability of any particular constitutional procedure to effect secession unless and until sufficiently clear facts exist to squarely raise an issue for judicial determination.*[94]

This is an important point, because it demonstrates that the Court does consider the issue of the applicability of a given amendment procedure to be a legal question that would be appropriate for the Court to answer, if and when a sufficient set of facts were to develop to warrant the determination of the issue. In other words, this is clearly an area in which the Court will retain its supervisory role, if ever it needs to be exercised in the future.

The "Principle of Effectivity"

Finally, before closing its opinion on Question 1, the Court examined the potential application of the "principle of effectivity" to the question. The *amicus curiae* had argued that "[l]e principe d'effectivité du droit international

---

the 7/50 formula that applied, rather than unanimity. The Ad Hoc Committee submitted that if any express procedure at all governed, it was s. 41, or alternatively, s. 38. Guy Bertrand argued emphatically that Question 1 required the Court to examine all the amendment procedures set out in Part V (not just s. 45, as the Attorney General of Canada had submitted) and that a complete response to the first question necessitated an analysis of ss. 38, 41, and 43 in order to clarify the law in this regard. Mr. Bertrand argued that s. 41 applied, or in the alternative, s. 38, and that s. 43 would also be called into play to effect border changes with neighbouring provinces.

[93] Factum of the Attorney General of Canada (filed 28 February 1997), paras. 116–119; Reply factum of the A.G. Canada (15 January 1998) paras. 40–47; Written Response of the A.G. Canada to Questions from the Supreme Court (6 March 1998), paras. 68–71. One group of interveners who supported the Attorney General of Canada's submission on this issue was Singh *et al.*: "It is not necessary, for present purposes [...] to decide which one or more constitutionally-prescribed methods could be employed to enact, *lawfully*, the substance or the terms of such a [secessionary] measure. (Much would depend on the *actual terms* in which a constitutional amendment was framed.)" Singh *et al.*, factum, para. 20; emphasis in original.

[94] *Reference re Secession of Quebec*, *supra*, para. 105; emphasis added.

transcendera le droit canadien"[95] or, alternatively, that the "principe d'effectivité" forms part of Canadian constitutional law itself, and that it would apply to a declaration of independence by the Quebec government or its institutions.[96]

The Attorney General of Canada argued that "effectivité" under international law is the acknowledgement of a factual situation that can exist only at the end of a period, and of a process, the legality of which was the very subject of Question 1.

> The position of the Attorney General of Canada is that the Constitution of Canada is not in abeyance while attempts are being made to create "effectivities." [...] Most importantly, the use of the "principe d'effectivité" to displace the terms of the Constitution would result in a legal vacuum and consequently, a flagrant conflict with one of the most fundamental constitutional principles of all—the rule of law.[97]

The Supreme Court agreed that the principle of effectivity had no application to the issues raised by Question 1. A unilateral declaration of independence leading to *de facto* secession is not a legal secession, even if, assuming the existence of effective control of the territory over a period of time, the revolutionary régime is eventually recognized as a sovereign state.

> *It was suggested* before us *that the National Assembly, legislature or government of Quebec could unilaterally effect* the *secession* of that province from Canada, *but it was not suggested that they might do so as a matter of law*: rather, it was contended that they simply could do so *as a matter of fact*. Although under the Constitution there is no right to pursue secession *unilaterally*, that is secession without principled negotiation, this does not rule out the possibility of an unconstitutional declaration of secession leading to a *de facto* secession. The ultimate success of such a secession would be dependent on effective control of a territory and recognition by the international community. The principles governing secession at international law are discussed in our answer to Question 2.[98]

The Court was emphatic in rejecting the idea that the "alleged principle of effectivity" could ever justify, in law, an illegal act of unilateral secession.

> In our view, the alleged principle of effectivity has *no constitutional or legal status* in the sense that it does not provide an *ex ante* explanation or justification for an act. *In essence, acceptance of a principle of effectivity would be tantamount to accepting that the National Assembly, legislature or government of Quebec may act without regard to the law, simply because it asserts the power to do so.* So viewed, the suggestion is that the National Assembly, legislature or government of Quebec could purport to secede the province unilaterally from Canada *in disregard of Canadian and international law*. It is further suggested that

---

[95] Factum of the *amicus curiae*, para. 114.

[96] *Id.*, paras. 115, 130–138.

[97] Reply factum of the A.G. Canada (15 January 1998), paras. 55 and 62; and see paras. 63–66.

[98] *Reference re Secession of Quebec, supra,* para. 106; emphasis added.

if the secession bid was successful, a new legal order would be created in that province, which would then be considered an independent state.

> *Such a proposition is an assertion of fact, not a statement of law.* It may or may not be true; in any event it is irrelevant to the questions of law before us. *If,* on the other hand, *it is put forward as an assertion of law, then it simply amounts to the contention that the law may be broken as long as it can be broken successfully. Such a notion is contrary to the rule of law, and must be rejected.*[99]

The much-vaunted effectivity principle[100] is thus no legal principle at all in the context of unilateral secession, because it amounts to accepting that the National Assembly, legislature, or government of Quebec "may act without regard to the law, simply because it asserts the power to do so," "in disregard of Canadian and international law"; and it "amounts to the contention that the law may be broken as long as it can be broken successfully." This proposition "is contrary to the rule of law, and must be rejected." These words of the Supreme Court of Canada bear repeating and should put to rest, once and for all, the claim put forward by the Attorney General of Quebec in the *Bertrand* case that unilateral secession is anything more than an illegal and revolutionary act—the exercise of unbridled, arbitrary power without the sanction or authority of law.

Question 2: Position of the Attorney General of Canada

The second Reference question reads as follows:

> Does international law give the National Assembly, legislature or government of Quebec the right to effect the secession of Quebec from Canada unilaterally? In this regard, is there a right to self-determination under international law that would give the National Assembly, legislature or government of Quebec the right to effect the secession of Quebec from Canada unilaterally?

The Attorney General of Canada submitted that international law, and in particular the right of self-determination of peoples under international law, gives no right to the National Assembly, legislature, or government of Quebec to effect the unilateral secession of Quebec from Canada. The right of self-determination under international law has both an external and an internal aspect. In neither respect does it involve any right to unilateral secession from an independent democratic state such as Canada. Outside the context of colonies, and possibly peoples under alien denomination or subject to gross oppression, the right of external self-determination can

---

[99] *Id.*, paras. 107 and 108; emphasis added.

[100] See Henri Brun and Guy Tremblay, *Droit constitutionel*, 3d edition (Cowansville, Quebec: Yvon Blais, 1997), at pp. 71–73, where the "principe d'effectivité" has essentially replaced "auto-détermination" (compare with 2d ed., 1990, at pp. 236–237) as a possible legal justification for Quebec secession. Professor Brun acted as part of the legal team advising counsel for the Attorney General of Quebec during the hearing of the A.G. Quebec's motion to dismiss the *Bertrand* case before Pidgeon J. of the Superior Court in May 1996.

only be exercised by the entire people of a state In independent states, the external aspect of the right of self-determination is the right of the people of a state to determine, without external interference, their form of government and international status. This right is exercised fully by all Canadians, including Quebecers, within Canada.

The internal aspect of the right of self-determination involves the right of the people of the state to a government representing the whole of that people on a basis of full equality. Quebecers, along with all Canadians, participate fully in their governmental institutions, federal and provincial, on a basis of full equality and thereby exercise the right of self-determination in its internal aspect. In a state such as Canada in which the government represents the whole people on a basis of full equality, the principle of respect for territorial integrity under international law sets the limit for the exercise of the right of self-determination, and there is no right to unilateral secession from such a state.[101]

The *amicus curiae* had argued that because international law does not prohibit secession, "celle-ci fait l'objet d'un droit, au sens courant du terme."[102] The *amicus curiae* maintained that the term "the right to effect the secession of Quebec" in Question 2 should be interpreted "au sens de privilège, de permission ou de possibilité de faire légalement sécession."[103]

The Attorney General of Canada replied that the statement that international law permits secession was misleading, because it implied that international law contains a prescriptive rule authorizing or approving secession. Except in extraordinary circumstances, which all agreed had no application in this case, there is no such rule, and in fact none of the experts retained by the *amicus curiae* had suggested that there was. The fact that international law does not prohibit the secession of groups within existing states is a necessary consequence of the fact that international law generally does not address the conduct of entities that are not subjects of international law, nor does it attempt to regulate all human affairs. Secession, as Professor Crawford explained, "is one of a myriad of activities that are referred to the domestic jurisdiction of the state concerned."[104] The "soft" right or "privilege" theory advocated by the *amicus curiae* would mean that criminal or egregiously immoral conduct outside the purview of international law—and therefore not *prohibited* by international law—would be characterized as a "right" or "privilege" under international law. The theory would also eliminate the generally accepted and legally crucial distinction between situations where independence may indeed amount to a genuine right (colonies, situations of gross oppression) and situations where it is merely a possible factual outcome to a secessionary movement. Professor Franck, one of the

---

[101] Factum of the Attorney General of Canada (28 February 1997), paras. 121 *et seq.* (Overview).

[102] Factum of the *amicus curiae*, para. 79.

[103] *Id.*, para. 80.

[104] James Crawford, Experts' Reply Report (A.G. Canada), para. 14.

prominent experts engaged by the *amicus curiae*, had himself admitted that the "international system does not recognize a general right of secession" and that,

> [w]hatever the meaning of the admittedly continuing right of self-determination, it has not been endowed by States in texts or practice with anything remotely like an internationally validated *right*, accruing to every secession-minded people anywhere, to secede territorially, at will, from established States that are members in good standing in the international community.[105]

Question 2: Opinion of the Supreme Court of Canada

The Supreme Court of Canada began its substantive analysis of the issue by stating that

> It is clear that international law does not specifically grant component parts of sovereign states the legal right to secede unilaterally from their "parent" state. This is acknowledged by the experts who provided their opinions on behalf of both the *amicus curiae* and the Attorney General of Canada.[106]

In the absence of "specific authorization" for unilateral secession, proponents of such a right at international law attempt to base their argument on

1. the proposition that unilateral secession is not specifically prohibited and therefore is inferentially permitted; or

2. on the implied duty of states to recognize the legitimacy of secession effected through the exercise of the international law right of "a people" to self-determination.

Dealing first with the argument based on the absence of a specific prohibition, the Court noted that international law "contains neither a right of unilateral secession nor the explicit denial of such a right, although such a denial is, to some extent, implicit in the exceptional circumstances required for secession to be permitted under the right of a people to self-determination." The Court emphasized that international law "places great importance on the territorial integrity of nation states and, by and large, leaves the creation of a new state to be determined by the domestic law of the existing state of which the seceding entity presently forms a part."

> Where, as here, unilateral secession would be incompatible with the domestic Constitution, international law is likely to accept that conclusion subject to the right of peoples to self-determination.[107]

---

[105] Thomas M. Franck, *General Course in Public International Law*, Académie de Droit International, Recueil de cours, 1993-III, tome 240, pp. 143, 140 (emphasis in original).

[106] *Reference re Secession of Quebec, supra*, para. 111.

[107] *Id.*, para. 112.

Self-Determination and Territorial Integrity

Turning then to the right of a people to self-determination, the Court stated that the right is "so widely recognized" in international instruments that it is considered to be "a general principle of international law." The Court undertook a review of some of the basic international instruments and conventions that recognize the right of self-determination, beginning with Articles 1 and 55 of the *Charter of the United Nations*, Article 1 of the U.N.'s *International Covenant on Civil and Political Rights* and the *International Covenant on Economic, Social and Cultural Rights*, the U.N. General Assembly's *Declaration on Principles of International Law concerning Friendly Relations and Co-operation among States* and the *Declaration on the Occasion of the Fiftieth Anniversary of the United Nations*, as well as documents such as the Helsinki *Final Act of the Conference on Security and Co-operation in Europe*.[108]

The Court underlined that international law "expects that the right of self-determination will be exercised by peoples within the framework of existing sovereign states and consistently with the maintenance of the territorial integrity of those states," barring certain "exceptional circumstances."[109]

The right to self-determination is granted to "peoples" in international law, although the exact meaning of the word "people" in this context is still uncertain. It is clear, however, the Court stated, that a "people" does not necessarily mean the whole of a state's population, and may include only a portion of that population.[110] The Attorney General of Canada had submitted that "there clearly exists a Canadian people corresponding to the entire population of Canada as is the case for other existing States,"[111] and that given the marked tendency in international law towards a broader conception of "peoples" in the context of the *internal* aspect of self-determination, "[c]learly there is a Quebec people in a sociological, historical and political sense, as there may also be other groups, living in Quebec and elsewhere in Canada, that constitute a people in that sense."[112]

> There is no conflict in possessing a shared identity, both as a member of a distinctive people, society or community within Canada, and as a member of the Canadian people as a whole. Indeed, these multiple characteristics enhance the Canadian identity, rather than diminish it.[113]

---

[108] *Id.*, paras. 114–121.

[109] Para. 122.

[110] Para. 124.

[111] Reply of the A.G. Canada to Written Responses of the *Amicus Curiae* (13 March 1998), para. 24.

[112] Reply factum of the A.G. Canada (15 January 1998), para. 91.

[113] Reply of the A.G. Canada to Written Responses of the *Amicus Curiae* (13 March 1998), para. 21. The *amicus curiae* had argued, *inter alia*, that there is no Canadian people. The Attorney General of Canada replied (para. 20): "The *amicus curiae*'s contention that there are Aboriginal peoples, a Quebec people, an English-Canadian people, and an Acadian people— *but no Canadian people*—flies in the face of logic, Canadian law and Canada's social reality.

The Court stated that "[w]hile much of the Quebec population certainly shares many of the characteristics (such as a common language and culture) that would be considered in determining whether a specific group is a 'people,' as do other groups within Quebec and/or Canada," it was unnecessary to explore the legal characterization of the term "peoples" to answer Question 2. So too, the Court said, it was unnecessary to determine "whether, should a Quebec people exist within the definition of public international law, such a people encompasses the entirety of the provincial population or just a portion thereof." Nor was it necessary to examine "the position of the aboriginal population of Quebec." This was because, as the Court ruled,

> whatever be the correct application of the definition of people(s) in this context, their right of self-determination *cannot* in present circumstances *be said to ground a right to unilateral secession.*[114]

In examining the scope of the right to self-determination, the Court was at pains to emphasize that the right is "normally fulfilled through *internal* self-determination—a people's pursuit of its political, economic, social and cultural development within the framework of an existing state," and that a right to "*external* self-determination (which in this case potentially takes the form of the assertion of a right to unilateral secession) arises in only the most extreme of cases and, even then, under carefully defined circumstances."[115]

The Court reiterated its earlier statement that the principle of self-determination in international law "has evolved within a framework of respect for the territorial integrity of existing states." The various international instruments supporting the existence of a people's right to self-determination, such as the *Declaration on Friendly Relations*, the *Vienna Declaration*, and the *Declaration on the Occasion of the Fiftieth Anniversary of the United Nations*, for example, "also contain parallel statements supportive of the conclusion that the exercise of such a right must be sufficiently limited to prevent threats to an existing state's territorial integrity or the stability of relations between sovereign states."[116]

The Court also underlined, for emphasis, the commitment to the principle of the territorial integrity, political independence, and unity of States contained in the *Helsinki Final Act*, and its stipulation that

---

It ignores the fact that under the Constitution, the Parliament of Canada represents the whole of the people of Canada. It ignores the existence of French-speaking Canadians outside Quebec (other than the Acadians) who have constitutional rights that protect their language and culture. It ignores the fact that most English-*speaking* Canadians are not 'English Canadians' in terms of their origin. It ignores the contribution to Canada of the multicultural heritage of Canadians, and it ignores the very meaning and purpose inherent in Canadian citizenship, which grants, to each individual Canadian, membership and participation in a people and in a polity the whole of which is greater than the sum of its parts."

[114] *Reference re Secession of Quebec, supra.,* para. 125; emphasis added.

[115] *Id.,* para. 126; emphasis in original.

[116] Paras. 127, 128, and 129 of the reasons for judgment.

> No actions or situations in contravention of this principle [of territo-
> rial integrity] will be recognized as legal by the participating States.[117]

The Court closed its review of the international instruments by concluding:

> *There is no necessary incompatibility between the maintenance of the
> territorial integrity of existing states, including Canada, and the right
> of a "people" to achieve a full measure of self-determination.* A state
> whose government represents the whole of the people or peoples resident
> within its territory, on a basis of equality and without discrimination,
> and respects the principles of self-determination in its own internal
> arrangements, is entitled to the protection under international law of
> its territorial integrity.[118]

Thus, the right to self-determination at international law generally "operates within the overriding protection granted to the territorial integrity of
'parent' states."[119] Nonetheless, peoples under colonial rule or foreign occupation may exercise an *external* right of self-determination that, in the
context of the Reference, "would potentially mean secession."

> The right of colonial peoples to exercise their right to self-determina-
> tion by breaking away from the "imperial" power is now undisputed,
> but is irrelevant to this Reference.

> The other clear case where a right to external self-determination
> accrues is where a people is subject to alien subjugation, domination or
> exploitation outside a colonial context.[120]

The Court then suggested a third possible circumstance in which the
"right to self-determination may ground a right to unilateral secession":

> [T]he underlying proposition is that, when a people is blocked from the
> meaningful exercise of its right to self-determination internally, it is
> entitled, as a last resort, to exercise it by secession.[121]

The Court stated that "[w]hile it remains unclear whether this third
proposition actually reflects an established international law standard, it is
unnecessary for present purposes to make that determination."

> Even assuming that the third circumstance is sufficient to create a
> right to unilateral secession under international law, the current Quebec
> context cannot be said to approach such a threshold. As stated by the
> *amicus curiae,* Addendum to the factum of the *amicus curiae,* at paras.
> 15–16:
>
> > [TRANSLATION] 15. The Quebec people is not the victim of attacks
> > on its physical existence or integrity, or of a massive violation of

---

117 Cited in para. 129 of the Court's reasons; underlining by the Court.

118 Para. 130; emphasis added.

119 Para. 131.

120 Paras. 132 and 133.

121 Para. 134.

its fundamental rights. The Quebec people is manifestly not, in the opinion of the *amicus curiae*, an oppressed people.[122] [...]

The population of Quebec cannot plausibly be said to be denied access to government. Quebecers occupy prominent positions within the government of Canada. Residents of the province freely make political choices and pursue economic, social and cultural development within Quebec, across Canada, and throughout the world. The population of Quebec is equitably represented in legislative, executive and judicial institutions. In short, to reflect the phraseology of the international documents that address the right to self-determination of peoples, Canada is a "sovereign and independent state conducting itself in compliance with the principle of equal rights and self-determination of peoples and thus possessed of a government representing the whole people belonging to the territory without distinction."[123]

The Court also dismissed arguments that the failure to enact constitutional amendments of the type envisaged by the *Meech Lake Constitutional Accord* has blocked meaningful exercise of the right to self-determination for Quebecers.

The continuing failure to reach agreement on amendments to the Constitution, while a matter of concern, does not amount to a denial of self-determination. In the absence of amendments to the Canadian Constitution, we must look at the constitutional arrangements presently in effect, and we cannot conclude under current circumstances that those arrangements place Quebecers in a disadvantaged position within the scope of the international law rule.[124]

---

[122] Para. 135 of the reasons for judgment. Para. 16 of the addendum to the factum of the *amicus curiae*, also cited by the Court in para. 135 of its opinion in the Reference, reads as follows: "For close to 40 of the last 50 years, the Prime Minister of Canada has been a Quebecer. During this period, Quebecers have held from time to time all the most important positions in the federal Cabinet. During the 8 years prior to June 1997, the Prime Minister and the Leader of the Official Opposition in the House of Commons were both Quebecers. At present, the Prime Minister of Canada, the Right Honourable Chief Justice and two other members of the Court, the Chief of Staff of the Canadian Armed Forces and the Canadian ambassador to the United States, not to mention the Deputy Secretary-General of the United Nations, are all Quebecers. The international achievements of Quebecers in most areas of human endeavour are too numerous to list. Since the dynamism of the Quebec people has been directed toward the business sector, it has been clearly successful in Quebec, the rest of Canada and abroad."

[123] Para. 136 of the reasons for judgment. All of this is consistent with the position taken by the Attorney General of Canada: "[T]here can be no doubt that the province of Quebec is not a colony. Nor, obviously, is the province of Quebec subject to alien domination, that is, domination or occupation by a foreign state. The province of Quebec is an integral part of Canada and the population of Quebec participates in the Canadian constitutional system on a basis of full and complete equality. [...] Neither the province of Quebec nor its population suffers gross oppression. Quebecers can freely make their own political choices through both their federal and their provincial governmental institutions. As well, Quebecers can pursue their economic, social and cultural development through those same federal and provincial governmental institutions. [...]" Factum of the A.G. Canada (28 February 1997), paras. 190–191 *et seq.*

[124] Para. 137 of the reasons for judgment. See, for an example of this argument, Daniel Turp, "Le droit à la secession : l'expression du principe démocratique," in A.-G. Gagnon and F. Rocher, eds., *Réplique aux détracteurs de la souveraineté* (Montréal: vlb éditeur, 1992) 49 at pp. 57–58. This argument was refuted by the Attorney General of Canada in para. 196 of the factum.

The Court summarized its findings on the right of self-determination at international law by stating that it "only generates, at best, a right to external self-determination in situations of former colonies; where a people is oppressed, as for example under foreign military occupation; or where a definable group is denied meaningful access to government to pursue their political, economic, social and cultural development."

> Such exceptional circumstances are manifestly inapplicable to Quebec under existing conditions. Accordingly, *neither the population of the province of Quebec*, even if characterized in terms of "people" or "peoples," *nor its representative institutions*, the National Assembly, the legislature or government of Quebec, *possess a right, under international law, to secede unilaterally from Canada.*[125]

The Court acknowledged the importance of the submissions made by a number of interveners in relation to "the rights and concerns of aboriginal peoples in the event of a unilateral secession" including "the appropriate means of defining the boundaries of a seceding Quebec with particular regard to the Northern lands occupied largely by aboriginal peoples." However, the Court stated that in light of its finding that there is no right of Quebec or its population to unilateral secession, either under the Constitution of Canada or at international law, but rather that "a clear democratic expression of support for secession would lead under the Constitution to negotiations in which aboriginal interests would be taken into account," it was not necessary to explore the concerns of aboriginal people further in the Reference.[126]

The "Effectivity" Principle

The Court returned, in the context of Question 2, to the "effectivity" argument that had been advanced by the *amicus curiae* as a basis for a right of unilateral secession. The argument here was that while international law may not provide the foundation for a right to unilateral secession for Quebec,

---

[125] Para. 138 of the reasons for judgment. "Force est donc de constater, très fermement, qu'il n'y a rien, dans le droit international contemporain, qui puisse servir de fondement à un quelconque droit à l'indépendance des peuples non coloniaux, sauf, peut-être—sûrement même!—s'ils subissent une oppression dans le cadre de l'État auquel ils sont intégrés mais, même mes amis du Bloc Québécois les plus enthousiastes n'ont jamais réussi à me convaincre que le Québec soit, de près ou de loin, dans une telle situation." Alain Pellet, "La Souveraineté et l'auto-détermination—processus et conditions—quelques remarques d'internationaliste," in Canadian Bar Association, *The Act Respecting the Sovereignty of Quebec: Legal Perspectives* (Montreal: Conference of the Canadian Bar Association, 1995), at p. 5. "Although the inhabitants of Quebec—as much as all other inhabitants of Canada—may be deemed to have a continuing right to internal self-determination under the UN Covenants, they do not have a legal right, under international law, to secede from Canada. [...] The contrary view, put forward by a number of authors, mostly of Québécois origin, is not substantiated by any valid legal arguments. [...] [O]ne is confronted here with a political claim that is *totally unsupported by law* (although legal arguments are vociferously employed by the proponents of secession as a means of lending support to their political claims)." A. Cassese, *Self-Determination of Peoples: A Legal Reappraisal* (Cambridge: Cambridge University Press, 1995) at pp. 251, 253; emphasis in original.

[126] Para. 139 of the reasons for judgment.

international law does not prohibit secession and, as a matter of fact, international recognition of the new political reality would be achieved if it emerged through the effective control of the territory of what is actually the province of Quebec. The *amicus curiae* asserted that "une secession sera légale si elle est une réalité politique effective"[127] and that "quelles que soient les modalités de la secession, le critère déterminant est la constatation d'une souveraineté effective."[128]

The Attorney General of Canada submitted that the *amicus curiae*'s argument was fundamentally flawed.

> While international law may ultimately take account of a *fait accompli*, this is not the same thing as authorizing or approving the act before it becomes a *fait accompli*. An *ex post facto* accommodation is obviously not the same thing as an *ex ante* authorization. [...]
>
> "[L]'effectivité" is not a norm. It authorizes nothing and justifies nothing. In particular, it does not authorize secession as a matter either of right or of privilege.[129]

At the outset of its response to Question 2, the Court had noted that "the existence of a positive legal entitlement is quite different from a prediction that the law will respond after the fact to a then existing political reality. These two concepts examine different points in time. The questions posed to the Court address legal rights in advance of a unilateral act of purported secession."[130] "It is true," the Court now added, "that international law may well, depending on the circumstances, adapt to recognize a political and/or factual reality, regardless of the legality of the steps leading to its creation. However, as mentioned at the outset, effectivity, as such, does not have any real applicability to Question 2, which asks whether a *right* to unilateral secession exists."[131]

No one doubts, the Court continued, that legal consequences can flow from political facts, that sovereignty itself is a political fact, and that the secession of a province, "if successful in the streets," might indeed result in the creation of a new state. But international recognition "does not relate back to the date of secession to serve retroactively as a source of a 'legal' right to secede in the first place."

> Recognition occurs only after a territorial unit has been successful, as a political fact, in achieving succession.[132]

---

[127] Factum of the *amicus curiae*, para. 79.

[128] *Id.*, para. 86. In conclusion, the *amicus curiae* contended that the "principe d'effectivité" sufficed to warrant an affirmative response to Question 2 of the Reference (para. 91).

[129] Reply factum of the A.G. Canada (15 January 1998), paras. 77–86 ("A Fact Is Not a Right"). See also Professor Crawford's Reply Report (para. 8): "The question of the eventual effectiveness of an attempted secession is quite different from the question of whether an entity has a right to independence, for example by virtue of the right to self-determination."

[130] *Reference re Secession of Quebec, supra,* para. 110.

[131] *Id.*, para. 141.

[132] Para. 142.

The Court returned to its response in Question 1, where it had indicated that one of the legal norms to be considered by other states in granting or withholding recognition "is the legitimacy of the process by which the *de facto* secession is, or was, being pursued."

> As we indicated in our answer to Question 1, an emergent state that has disregarded legitimate obligations arising out of its previous situation can potentially expect to be hindered by that disregard in achieving international recognition, at least with respect to the timing of that recognition. On the other hand, compliance by the seceding province with such legitimate obligations would weigh in favour of international recognition. *The notion that what is not explicitly prohibited is implicitly permitted has little relevance where (as here) international law refers the legality of secession to the domestic law of the seceding state and the law of that state holds unilateral secession to be unconstitutional.*[133]

The Court did not shy away from underscoring the fact that a U.D.I. would amount to a revolution against the legal order of the existing state, and that no attempt to dress it up with the principle of "effectivity" would transform that revolution into a legal act.

> As a court of law, we are ultimately concerned only with legal claims. If the principle of "effectivity" is no more than that "successful revolution begets its own legality" (S.A. de Smith, "Constitutional Lawyers in Revolutionary Situations" (1968), 7 *West. Ont. L. Rev.* 93, at p. 96), it necessarily means that legality follows and does not precede the successful revolution. *Ex hypothesi*, the successful revolution took place outside the constitutional framework of the predecessor state, otherwise it would not be characterized as "a revolution". *It may be that a unilateral secession by Quebec would eventually be accorded legal status by Canada and other states, and thus give rise to legal consequences; but this does not support the more radical contention that subsequent recognition of a state of affairs brought about by a unilateral declaration of independence could be taken to mean that secession was achieved under colour of a legal right.*[134]

In closing, the Court returned once more to the rule of law and the *Manitoba Language Rights Reference*, which it had cited in the opening words of its opinion in the *Secession Reference*. The *amicus curiae* had argued that the Court, in the *Manitoba Language Rights Reference*, had invoked the rule of law principle to save Manitoba from the consequences of its unconstitutional actions in a manner similar to the way in which the operation of the principle of "effectivity" was alleged by the *amicus curiae* to operate, in that both principles "attempt to refashion the law to meet social reality."[135] The Attorney General of Canada had argued[136] that remedial

---

[133] Para. 143; emphasis added.

[134] Para. 144; emphasis added.

[135] Para. 145.

[136] Written Response of the A.G. Canada to Questions from the Supreme Court (6 March 1998), para. 42.

doctrines supporting the measures taken by the Court in the *Manitoba Language Rights Reference* to preserve the rule of law could not be invoked in advance to oust the Constitution. This would contravene the clear terms of s. 52 of the *Constitution Act, 1982*. The Court rejected the comparison advanced by the *amicus curiae* between the principle of the rule of law and that of "effectivity."

> [N]othing of our concern in the *Manitoba Language Rights Reference* about the severe practical consequences of unconstitutionality affected our conclusion that, as a matter of law, all Manitoba legislation at issue in that case was unconstitutional. The Court's declaration of unconstitutionality was clear and unambiguous. The Court's concern with maintenance of the rule of law was directed in its relevant aspect to the appropriate remedy, which in that case was to suspend the declaration of invalidity to permit appropriate rectification to take place.[137]

"The principle of effectivity," the Court continued, "operates very differently."

> It proclaims that an illegal act may eventually acquire legal status if, as a matter of empirical fact, it is recognized on the international plane.[138]

This is akin, for example, to the way a squatter eventually acquires title to land under the law of property.

> It is, however, quite another matter to suggest that a subsequent condonation of an initially illegal act retroactively creates a legal right to engage in the act in the first place. The broader contention is not supported by the international principle of effectivity or otherwise and must be rejected.[139]

Question 3

Question 3 in the Reference reads:

> In the event of a conflict between domestic and international law on the right of the National Assembly, legislature or government of Quebec to effect the secession of Quebec from Canada unilaterally, which would take precedence in Canada?

The Attorney General of Canada submitted that there is no conflict between domestic and international law because neither gives the National Assembly, legislature, or government of Quebec the right to effect the secession of Quebec from Canada unilaterally. However, if there were such a conflict, Canadian courts would be bound to apply domestic law in preference to international law. "Should the Court agree with this position [that there is no conflict], it would not be necessary for the Court to answer the question further than to state that there is no conflict."[140]

---

[137] Para. 145 of the reasons for judgment.

[138] Para. 146.

[139] *Ibid.*

[140] Factum of the A.G. Canada (28 February 1997), paras. 200–201. The full argument on the principles governing the application of international law in Canada is set out in paras.

This was the position adopted by the Court.

> In view of our answers to Questions 1 and 2, there is no conflict between domestic and international law to be addressed in the context of this Reference.[141]

Summary of Conclusions

The Court devoted the final paragraphs of its opinion to presenting a synthesis of the conclusions it had reached on the issues before it in the *Quebec Secession Reference*. Those conclusions are paraphrased and encapsulated below in this text in bullet form.

• This Reference involves ***momentous questions*** that go to the heart of our system of constitutional government.

• The Constitution is ***more than a written text;*** it embraces the global system of rules and principles that govern the exercise of constitutional authority.

• The ***underlying principles*** that animate the whole of our Constitution, including ***federalism, democracy, constitutionalism and the rule of law, and respect for minorities,*** must inform our overall appreciation of the constitutional rights and obligations that would come into play in the event that a clear majority of Quebecers votes on a clear question in favour of secession.[142]

• The Reference requires us to consider whether Quebec has a right to *unilateral* secession. Those who support such a right invoke the principle of democracy, but ***democracy means more than simple majority rule.*** Democracy exists in the larger context of other constitutional values.

• In the 131 years since Confederation, the people of the provinces and territories have created ***close ties of interdependence*** (economically, socially, politically, and culturally) ***based on shared values*** that include federalism, democracy, constitutionalism and the rule of law, and respect for minorities. A democratic decision of Quebec in favour of secession would put those relationships at risk.

• The Constitution assures ***order and stability.*** Secession under the Constitution could not be achieved ***unilaterally,*** that is, without principled negotiations with other participants in Confederation within the existing constitutional framework.[143]

• ***"The Constitution is not a straitjacket."*** Our constitutional history demonstrates periods of momentous and dramatic change.

202–209 of the factum. See also paras. 96–100 of the A.G. Canada's Reply factum (15 January 1998).

[141] *Reference re Secession of Quebec, supra,* para. 147.

[142] *Id.,* drawn from para. 148.

[143] From para. 149.

• Our democratic institutions accommodate a continuous process of discussion and evolution, reflected in the *right of each participant in the federation to initiate constitutional change.* This right implies a *reciprocal duty* to engage in discussions to address any legitimate initiative to change the constitutional order.

• While some recent attempts at constitutional amendment have faltered, a clear majority vote in Quebec on a clear question on secession would confer *democratic legitimacy* on the secession initiative that other participants in Confederation would have to recognize.[144]

• *Quebec could not* purport to invoke a right of self-determination to *dictate the terms of a proposed secession* to the other parties to the federation. The democratic vote, by however strong a majority, would have *no legal effect* on its own and could not push aside the principles of federalism and the rule of law, the rights of individuals and minorities, or the operation of democracy in other provinces or in Canada as a whole.

• On the other hand, the continued existence and operation of the Canadian constitutional order *could not be indifferent* to a clear expression of a clear majority of Quebecers that they no longer wish to remain in Canada. The other provinces and the federal government would have no basis to deny the *right* of the government of Quebec *to pursue secession* so long as Quebec respects the rights of others.

• Negotiations would address the potential act of secession as well as its possible terms should in fact secession proceed. There would be *no conclusions pre-determined by law* on any issue.

• Negotiations would need to address the interests of the other *provinces,* the *federal government, Quebec,* and indeed the *rights of all Canadians both within and outside Quebec,* and specifically the rights of *minorities.* "No one suggests it would be an easy set of negotiations."[145]

• Negotiations would require the reconciliation of rights and obligations between *two legitimate majorities,* i.e., the majority of the population of Quebec, and that of Canada as a whole.

• A political majority that does not act in accordance with the four underlying constitutional principles puts at risk the *legitimacy* of the exercise of its rights, and the ultimate acceptance of the result by the international community.[146]

• The role of the Court is to clarify the *legal framework* within which political decisions are to be taken under the Constitution, not to usurp the political forces that operate within that framework. The *obligations* are *binding* ones under the Constitution of Canada. However, it is for the

---

[144] Para. 150.

[145] Para. 151.

[146] Para. 152.

political actors to determine what constitutes "a *clear majority* on a *clear question*" in a future referendum. The context and process of any ensuing *negotiations* will also be for the political actors to settle, as is the reconciliation of the various legitimate constitutional interests. *To the extent issues* addressed in the course of negotiation are *political*, the *courts*, appreciating their proper role in the constitutional scheme, would have *no supervisory role.*

• Although much of the Quebec population shares much of the characteristics of a people, it is not necessary to decide whether that population is "a people" within the meaning of international law, because a right of secession arises only under the principle of *self-determination* of peoples at international law where a people is governed as part of a colonial empire; where a people is subject to alien subjugation, domination, or exploitation; and possibly where a people is denied any meaningful exercise of its right to self-determination within the state of which it forms a part.

• In other circumstances peoples are expected to achieve self-determination *within the framework* of their existing state.

• A state whose government represents the whole of the people or peoples resident within its territory, on a basis of equality and without discrimination, and respects the principles of self-determination in its internal arrangements, is entitled to maintain its *territorial integrity* under international law and to have that territorial integrity recognized by other states.

• Quebec *does not meet* the threshold of a colonial people or an oppressed people, nor can it be suggested that Quebecers have been denied meaningful access to government to pursue their political, economic, cultural, and social development.

• In the circumstances, the National Assembly, the legislature, or the government of Quebec *do not enjoy a right at international law* to effect the secession of Quebec unilaterally.[147]

• Although there is *no right, under the Constitution or at international law, to unilateral secession,* that is secession without negotiation on the basis discussed above, this does not rule out the possibility of an *unconstitutional declaration of secession* leading to a *de facto* secession.

• The ultimate success of such a secession would be dependent on recognition by the international community, which is likely to consider the *legality and legitimacy* of secession having regard to, among other facts, the conduct of Quebec and Canada, in determining whether to grant or withhold recognition.

• Such recognition, even if granted, *would not*, however, *provide any retroactive justification* for the act of secession, either under the Constitution of Canada or at international law.[148]

---

[147] Para. 154.

[148] Para. 155.

4

The Aftermath of the Reference and Lessons for the Future

Reaction to the Supreme Court's Reference Opinion

On August 20, 1998, shortly after the Reference opinion was issued by the Supreme Court, the Prime Minister of Canada released a statement in which he declared that the Court "has well served all Canadians by bringing clarity to certain fundamental rules which must guide our democratic life, even in dealing with the most difficult questions." The Government of Quebec's assertion of a right to effect Quebec's independence unilaterally "posed the most serious risk" for public order as well as the rights of citizens.

> The federal government had the responsibility to ask our highest court to clarify these fundamental questions and considered that it was best to do it in a period of calm, away from any referendums. [...]
>
> The Court's ruling is an important reminder of some basic elements of democratic life and civil order. It deserves the respect of all Canadians.[1]

The Minister of Justice and Attorney General of Canada, the Honourable Anne McLellan, stated that the Government was "pleased that the Court had recognized the clear legal nature of the questions posed."

> The Court acknowledged that the questions raise issues of fundamental public importance. Most importantly, the Court has underlined the importance of the rule of law as an essential underpinning of democracy. The Court has emphasized the importance and interdependence of the constitutional principles of federalism, democracy, constitutionalism and the rule of law, and respect for minorities. [...]
>
> The Court's emphasis on constitutional negotiations to achieve secession is also consistent with the Government of Canada's long-standing position. Under the Constitution, secession requires that an amendment be negotiated.[2]

The Minister of Justice also emphasized, as the Court did, that "the rule of law is the framework within which democracy operates."

---

[1] Statement by the Right Honourable Jean Chrétien, the Prime Minister of Canada, on the Supreme Court of Canada's Ruling in the Reference on Unilateral Secession; Office of the Prime Minister (20 August 1998), pp. 1–2.

[2] Statement by the Minister of Justice and Attorney General of Canada, the Honourable Anne McLellan, in Response to the Ruling of the Supreme Court (20 August 1998), pp. 1–2.

Democracy and the rule of law support and sustain each other. [...] It is the law that creates the framework within which the "sovereign will" is to be ascertained and implemented.[3]

The Minister of Intergovernmental Affairs, the Honourable Stéphane Dion, repeated that it was better to clarify "in an atmosphere of calm, rather than in the turbulent environment of a possible attempt at secession," whether the Government of Quebec had the right or authority to effect Quebec's independence unilaterally.

If a government attempted unilaterally to effect independence, many resulting issues would have inevitably have come before the courts. Are we to believe that no Quebecer would have gone to court to challenge a unilateral act designed to deprive him of his rights as a Canadian? [...] There are few things more dangerous in a democracy than a government that places itself above the law but continues to demand obedience of its citizens.[4]

The Court had confirmed in the Reference that the Government of Quebec has no constitutional power, or right at international law, to effect unilateral secession.

This means that the Government of Quebec is not in a position on its own to impose the process and terms of the break-up of Canada.

Secession would have to be negotiated, taking into account not just the logistical details of secession, but more importantly, the interests of the provinces, the federal government, Quebec, and the rights of all Canadians both within and outside Quebec, including minorities, as the Court had ruled.[5]

Our citizens are the big winners. The citizens of Quebec have had their right to remain part of Canada confirmed so long as they have not clearly indicated their desire to leave. In addition, they have obtained the assurance that they will not be held in Canada against their clearly expressed will.[6]

---

[3] *Id.*, at p. 2.

[4] Statement by the Honourable Stéphane Dion, President of the Privy Council and Minister of Intergovernmental Affairs, in Response to the Ruling of the Supreme Court (20 August 1998), pp. 2–3.

[5] *Ibid.* Minister Dion noted that this was "the position I presented as well in my letters to Prime Minister Bouchard and his Ministers." This was an allusion to four letters the Minister had written to his Quebec counterparts on August 11, 26, and 28, 1997 and November 19, 1997, respectively, dealing not only with the legal but the political, philosophical and practical consequences of a unilateral declaration of independence, both domestically and internationally. In the English version of his letter of August 26, 1997, for example, Mr. Dion noted that "in all cases where a referendum has been held, it has always been to confirm the existence of a clear consensus. [...] Our governments would be acting irresponsibly if they tried to negotiate a break-up without solid information that this is truly what Quebecers want." The "Dion Letters" garnered a lot of media attention in Quebec and the rest of Canada, and prompted the Quebec government to debate the issues in a written reply and in oral reaction. Mr. Dion would soon write another letter, in response to Premier Bouchard's statement following the Reference opinion (discussed *infra*).

[6] *Id.*; p. 3 of Minister Dion's statement.

The initial reaction from the Government of Quebec came from Ministers Brassard and Landry, both of whom found aspects of the Court's opinion to be "intéressants," particularly the recognition by the Court of the legitimacy of the secessionist option and the obligation to negotiate should that option obtain a clear majority on a clear question.[7] The detailed reaction to the judgment was given the next day, by the Premier of Quebec. In a televised statement that in substance was favourable to the judgment, but in form had not unburdened itself of the heavy and one-sided rhetoric that had characterized the Government of Quebec's previous interventions on the issue, Mr. Bouchard stated that

> La Cour a démontré que l'argumentaire d'Ottawa ne résiste pas à l'analyse et a frappé au coeur même du discours fédéraliste traditionnel.
>
> Globalement, les fédéralistes nous ont affirmé depuis deux ans que la souveraineté est un problème juridique qui relève des tribunaux et du droit. Les juges fédéraux les ont contredits. Après avoir répondu, de façon parfaitement prévisible et prévue, aux questions réductrices posées par le gouvernement fédéral, la Cour a affirmé, d'un bout à l'autre de son avis, le caractère politique de la démarche qui serait légitimement enclenchée par un référendum québécois sur la souveraineté.[8]

This ignored entirely the Court's conclusions that the questions put to the Court "may clearly be interpreted as directed to legal issues," were "legal questions touching and concerning the future of the Canadian federation," and were ones that raised "issues of fundamental public importance."[9] It also ignored the Court's clear statement, at the outset of its analysis of the operation of constitutional principles in the secession context, that

> Secession is a legal act as much as a political one.[10]

Premier Bouchard went on to list the five "mythes fédéralistes" that in his view were buried by the Court in the Reference judgment: (1) "que le projet de souveraineté n'est pas légitime"; (2) "que si les Québécoises et les Québécois disaient Oui, le Canada refuserait de négocier"; (3) "que, si les négociations finissaient par avoir lieu après un Oui, elles porteraient, non sur la souveraineté, mais sur un renouvellement du fédéralisme"; (4) "[qu']après un Oui, en cas d'impasse des négociations, les Québécoises et les Québécois

---

[7] "'The Supreme Court has recognized the democratic legitimacy of both the option and the process leading to the realization of the sovereignty project, whereby a majority Yes vote in a referendum would imply that the federal government and the other provinces would have the obligation to recognize the majority vote,' Mr. Brassard said in a news conference yesterday." *Globe & Mail*: "Ruling Legitimized Sovereignty Drive, PQ Leaders Say" (21 August 1998). "Cet aspect de l'obligation de négocier est intéressant pour nous." *La Presse:* "« Ça peut changer l'atmosphère au Canada », croit Landry" (21 August 1998).

[8] Notes pour une déclaration liminaire du premier ministre du Québec, M. Lucien Bouchard, au lendemain de l'avis de la Cour suprême du Canada sur le renvoi du gouvernement fédéral, à Québec le 21 août 1998; p. 1.

[9] *Reference re Secession of Quebec, supra,* reasons for judgment, paras. 28, 20, and 31.

[10] *Id.*, para. 83.

sont prisonniers du Canada, ils ne peuvent pas sortir"; (5) "que le gouvernement fédéral devrait être impliqué dans la rédaction et dans l'adoption de
la question ou dans la fixation d'un nouveau seuil de majorité."[11]

Mr. Bouchard ended his declaration by stating that

> [d]e plus en plus de femmes et d'hommes du Québec en concluront
> que le temps est bientôt venu de décider, une fois pour toutes, de
> mettre un terme à nos querelles insolubles avec le Canada, de bâtir ici
> le pays du Québec, et de négocier avec nos voisins, une relation d'égal
> à égal, mutuellement bénéfique.[12]

The Prime Minister of Canada responded with his own televised address
the same day, noting, amongst other things, that the Court's decision demonstrated that the unilateral declaration of independence "que l'actuel
gouvernement du Québec avait dans sa poche arrière avant le dernier référendum" was contrary to Canadian law and basic democratic principles. As well:

> Une telle déclaration unilatérale d'indépendence ne peut s'appuyer sur
> le droit international. Voilà qui enterre l'un des principaux mythes que
> les partisans de la séparation ont tenté de créer au fil des ans.[13]

The Prime Minister also emphasized the Court's finding, in para. 87 of
its opinion, that for the referendum to be taken as an expression of the
democratic will, the result "must be free of ambiguity both in terms of the
question asked and in terms of the support it achieves."

> Cet élément est très important. [...] Cela signifie que l'époque des
> « astuces » et des « questions gagnantes » est terminée. [...] La Cour
> suprême nous dit également que la démocratie nécessite une négociation
> de bonne foi lorsqu'une majorité claire des Québécois exprime
> clairement son désir de ne plus faire partie du Canada.[14]

On August 25, 1998, the federal Minister of Intergovernmental Affairs
wrote to the Premier of Quebec in response to the latter's interpretation of
the Supreme Court's opinion in the Reference, which Mr. Dion described
as a selective "game of light and shadows".[15]

> The government of Canada has, of course, declared itself bound by all
> aspects of the ruling. You, on the other hand, only recognize its legal
> validity for others and not for you or your government. You praise those

---

[11] Premier Bouchard's statement, *supra*.

[12] *Id.*, at p. 4.

[13] Déclaration du premier ministre du Canada (21 August 1998) reproduced in *Le Devoir*
under the headline "Fini les astuces!" (22 August 1998). Prior to tabling the Draft Bill, *An
Act respecting the sovereignty of Québec*, and the draft referendum question in December
1994, Premier Parizeau had told journalists that they would find what he was about to
announce to be quite "astucieux".

[14] *Ibid.*

[15] English translation of a letter by Minister Dion to Premier Bouchard, reproduced in the
Ottawa Citizen under the heading "Stop 'This Game of Light and Shadows,'" and in the
original French in *La Presse* under the title, "Dion réplique à Bouchard" (26 August 1998).

passages that interest you and ignore the content—however obvious—
of those passages that displease you.

It was precisely the obligation to negotiate that pleased you. [...]
There is, however, a point that cannot be ignored: given that this obligation is reciprocal, it would also be binding on you, much more so than
the negotiations you had in mind in case of a referendum victory in 1995.

Mr. Dion went on to list three fundamental differences between what
was envisaged by the Government of Quebec in 1995 and what was now
required with respect to the obligation to negotiate: (1) negotiations would
be conditional on clear support for secession ("You can no longer claim to
be the sole arbiter of the clarity of the question and the majority"); (2) the
negotiation of secession would have to take place within the constitutional
framework ("no one can now ignore that such an attempt at unilateral
secession [as contemplated in Bill 1] would have had no legal basis"); and
(3) the content of the negotiations on secession could not be dictated per-
emptorily ("You can no longer claim that you alone would determine what
would be on the negotiating table").

In short, the obligation to negotiate secession, to which the Supreme
Court has now given a constitutional dimension, itself depends on
clear support for secession, respect for the constitutional framework
and a great deal of good faith. If your government fails to observe
these principles of clarity, legality and good faith, the constitutional
obligation to negotiate no longer holds.

Negotiations on secession based on the clear support of Quebecers
conducted legally, and with a concern for justice for all. This is the
only way to achieve independence for Quebec. The time for stratagems
and "winning" tricks is over.

The Court's position in the *Quebec Secession Reference* engendered a great
deal of other immediate political and public reaction,[16] editorial commentary,[17]

---

[16] A scan of some of the headlines in the newspaper on the day after the judgment,
August 21, 1998, conveys a quick sense of the range of reaction: "Feds Got All the Answers
They Wanted": Paul Wells (analysis), *The Gazette*; "Un avis plutôt favorable aux
souverainistes, selon les constitutionalistes": Michel Venne (analysis), *Le Devoir*; "Ruling Is
Prudent, Legal Scholars Say": *Ottawa Citizen*; "Federalist, Separatist Camps Can Both Claim
Victory": Joan Bryden (analysis), *Ottawa Citizen*; "L'avis embêtera les purs et durs des deux
camps": *Le Droit*; "Magnificent Judgment on Secession a Model for the World": William
Johnson (column), *Financial Post*; "Bouchard Wins Upper Hand," L. Ian MacDonald (column),
The Gazette; "Les experts réagissent de façon positive": *La Presse*; "Les autochtones
applaudissent"; "Les anglophones sont contents"; "Guy Bertrand jubile"; "Aucun camp ne
gagne, croit Jean-Claude Rivest": *Le Devoir*; "Claude Ryan agréablement surpris": *Le Journal
de Montréal*; "Un jugement à la Solomon": *La Presse*; and on August 22, 1998, "Dion's Just
Rewards": Joan Bryden (analysis), *Ottawa Citizen*; "Bouchard et Chrétien heureux du
jugement": *La Presse*; "We Win, Both Claim": *The Gazette*; "Bouchard applaudit le jugement":
Le Soleil; "Le froid réalisme": Manon Cornellier (analysis), *Le Devoir*.

[17] The editorials on August 21, 1998 included the following: "Common Sense from the
Court": *The Gazette*; "La victoire du bon sens": *La Presse*; "Advantage Bouchard": *Ottawa
Citizen*; "Confederation Is Voluntary": *Globe & Mail*; "Quebec Can't Dictate Terms of Secession": *Toronto Star*; "B comme dans boomerang": *Le Devoir*; "Future of This Country Belongs
to All Canadians": *Financial Post*.

and legal and political analysis,[18] most of it very favourable to the careful balance struck by the Court on the legal issues, rights, and interests of all concerned. There were also, predictably, dissenting voices at both ends of the spectrum,[19] as well as some sober and iconoclastic second thought[20] in the days and weeks after the judgment.

The leader of the Bloc Québécois, Gilles Duceppe, M.P., whose caucus had demonstrated against the Reference on the steps of the Supreme Court building at the outset of the hearing, now found the opinion of the Court to be worthy of five pages of detailed comments, which he included in a letter to the members of all legislative assemblies in Canada.

> Peu importe nos opinions respectives à l'époque du renvoi par le gouverne-ment fédéral, le présent avis aura une portée politique majeure pour l'ensemble des provinces canadiennes. [...]
>
> Cela étant dit, au-delà de nos divergences d'opinion, cet avis de la Cour suprême offre d'abord une occasion historique de renouer le dia-logue entre le Québec et le Canada en vue d'un nouveau partenariat. Comme j'ai eu la chance de le répéter dans chacune des provinces canadiennes au cours des derniers mois, une déclaration unilatérale d'indépendance n'est pas, et n'a jamais été, le premier choix des souverainistes québécois.[21]

For his own part, Mario Dumont, the leader of the Action Démocratique party, who, with the former leaders of the Parti Québécois and the Bloc Québécois, had signed the "tripartite agreement" in 1995 favouring a partner-ship with Canada but preserving potential recourse to a U.D.I., was of the view that the opinion of the Supreme Court of Canada in the Reference could, through the obligation to negotiate, open the door to major constitutional

---

[18] "A Wise Judgment": Julius H. Grey, *The Gazette* (22 August 1998); "The Supreme Court's Ruling—Putting Things Straight": Kenneth McRoberts; "The Court Reminds Us of Compromise": William Thorsell; *Globe & Mail* (21 August 1998).

[19] "How to Deny Quebec's Right to Self-Determination": Josée Legault, *Globe & Mail* (21 August 1998); "Courageous or Just 'Candy'?": *Toronto Star* (21 August 1998); "A Ticket to Separate": Ted Morton, *Ottawa Citizen* (22 August 1998); "Making It Up as They Go Along": Robert Martin, *The Gazette* (26 August 1998); "Down the Garden Path We Go": David Frum, *Ottawa Sun* (28 August 1998); "Une cour au service du gouvernement canadien": Michael Mandel, *Le Devoir* (1 October 1998); "La Cour suprême et la secession du Québec": Guy Laforest, *La Presse* (6 November 1998); "A Constitutional Time Bomb": Andrew Coyne, *National Post* (30 December 1998).

[20] "What If Voters Voted Clearly for Secession?": Claude Ryan, *Globe & Mail* (27 August 1998); "The Court's Supreme Paradox": William Watson, *The Gazette* (31 August 1998); "Une sécession légitime et réalisable ... en théorie"; "Une souveraineté systématiquement entravée en pratique": Jacques-Yvan Morin, *Le Devoir* (31 August and 1 September 1998); "Lettre ouverte aux juges de la Cour suprême"; "Et si les négociations échouaient?": Jacques Parizeau, *Le Devoir* (3 and 4 September 1998); "La Cour suprême a-t-elle voulu se « racheter » pour son attitude de 1982?": José Woehrling, *La Presse* (10 September 1998); "Le double rôle indissociable de la Cour suprême": Andrée Lajoie, *Le Devoir* (10 September 1998); "A Trump Card Handed to Bouchard": Norman Spector, *Globe & Mail* (24 September 1998).

[21] Lettre adressée à tous les député(e)s des assemblées législatives; Gilles Duceppe, député de Laurier-Sainte-Marie, Chef du Bloc Québécois (31 August 1998).

reform in Canada.[22] Mr. Dumont went so far as to introduce a private member's bill, entitled *An Act respecting the Québec proposal for constitutional peace*, which would have established a moratorium on any referendum concerning "a question or bill pertaining to Quebec sovereignty," and would have required the Government of Quebec, "in pursuance of the constitutional principle recognized in paragraphs 69 and 88 of the Supreme Court opinion appearing in the Schedule" to the proposed Act, to "put forward a proposal for constitutional peace" and "to propose the implementation of in-depth reform of the political and constitutional framework governing Québec society."[23]

The Supreme Court's opinion also prompted a great deal of public debate on the clarity of the referendum question and of the majority vote that would be needed to trigger the duty to negotiate. In his open letter to the Supreme Court following the Reference, former Premier Jacques Parizeau wrote:

> En 1980, nous voulions un mandat de négocier. En 1995, nous demandions l'autorisation de procéder à la souveraineté. [...]
>
> On nous a souvent dit que la question de 1995 n'était pas claire. C'est vrai, comme je l'ai souvent souligné, que la question que j'aurais voulu poser était la suivante: « *Voulez-vous que le Québec devienne un pays souverain en date du ... ?* » [...]
>
> Votre avis éclaircit bien des choses. [...]
>
> Alors, la question posée pourrait être à la fois simple et claire: « *Voulez-vous que le Québec devienne un pays souverain (ou indépendant)?* »[24]

Premier Bouchard himself had indicated, in an interview with *Le Devoir* and in a press conference after the Reference, that perhaps the quality and the clarity of the question might be improved in light of the Supreme Court's opinion:

> Il se pourrait qu'on trouve dans le jugement de la Cour suprême des éléments qui vont nous permettre d'ajouter encore à la qualité et à la clarté de la question.[25]

---

[22] "Dumont: « Il faut jouer à fond l'obligation de négocier »": *La Presse* (22 August 1998); "La Cour suprême a ouvert une nouvelle voie": *Le Devoir* (27 August 1998).

[23] Bill 399, *An Act respecting the Québec proposal for constitutional peace*, National Assembly, Second Session, Thirty-Fifth Legislature; introduced on October 21, 1998 by Mr. Mario Dumont, Member for Rivière-du-Loup; ss. 1, 2, and 3. The Bill, much along the lines of the Allaire Report, proposed an extensive reform of the federal–provincial division of powers (ss. 4–7), and measures relating to the economic union (s. 8), the federal spending power (s. 9), overlapping jurisdictions (s. 10), changes to the amending formula (s. 11), central institutions (ss. 12–13), and negotiation of the Quebec proposal (s. 14). The Bill died on the order paper at the end of the session, but newspaper reports indicated that Mr. Dumont might re-introduce it ("Dumont représentera son projet de loi sur la paix constitutionelle": *La Presse* (2 December 1998).

[24] "Lettre ouverte aux juges de la Cour suprême," *supra*, Jacques Parizeau, *Le Devoir* (3 September 1998); emphasis in original.

[25] "Bouchard promet une question plus claire": *Le Devoir* (28 August 1998); "Next Question Will Be Clearer: Bouchard": *The Gazette* (29 August 1998); "Question on Next Referendum Will Be Clearer, Bouchard Says": *Globe & Mail* (29 August 1998).

After Mr. Parizeau's letter appeared, Premier Bouchard stated that the former Premier's proposed referendum question merited consideration, as would other proposals.[26]

The issue of what would constitute a clear majority also received extensive coverage in the media after the Reference opinion.[27] Such questions defy legal analysis, as the Court said, and must ultimately be left to the political actors to assess and to evaluate.

The broad public reaction to the Supreme Court's opinion in the *Quebec Secession Reference* has now largely abated, but the political actors, legal practitioners, jurists, political scientists, and other interested segments of the Canadian polity will continue to examine the scope and impact of the judgment in the months and years to come.[28]

There is something remarkable to be said, however, about an opinion of the Supreme Court of Canada on Quebec secession (and the judges who crafted it) that could move a long-time *indépendantiste* like Pierre Bourgault to speak of "l'intelligence du texte, la profondeur des énoncés, la clarté du propos";[29] and that could prompt Professor Henri Brun, one of the legal advisors acting for the Attorney General of Quebec in the *Bertrand* case, and who had denounced the Reference on more than one occasion, to state:

---

[26] "La proposition de Parizeau mérite d'être regardée, estime Bouchard": *Le Devoir* (4 September 1998); "Bouchard prend acte de la suggestion de Parizeau": *La Presse* (4 September 1998). For an excellent analysis of the problems posed by the 1995 referendum question, which effectively asked two questions, one on sovereignty and one on partnership, but permitted only one response, see Jean-Pierre Derriennic, "Comment savoir si une question est claire": *Le Devoir* (8 September 1998) and *La Presse* (5 September 1998). Professor Derriennic suggests that an example of a clear question would be: "Voulez-vous que le Québec cesse de faire partie du Canada pour devenir un État indépendant?" He also suggests ways of asking a second question on partnership.

[27] Michel Venne makes an interesting argument when he states: "La cour s'abstient de déterminer le pourcentage du vote requis pour que la majorité soit considérée comme claire. Elle soutient que ce sont les acteurs politiques qui en décideront. Le gouvernement du Québec ne sera pas le seul juge. Québec a raison de dire que, sur le plan légal, la norme du 50% plus une voix est suffisante. Elle ne le serait certainement pas sur le plan politique car on ne fait pas naître un État indépendant sans un recomptage judiciaire. Il est toutefois impossible de fixer à l'avance un autre seuil sans accorder aux opposants un poids plus élevé qu'à ceux qui souhaitent l'indépendance du Québec et sans risquer de créer une situation chaotique si une majorité claire de Québécois votaient OUI mais qu'il ne manquait que quelques voix pour atteindre la nouvelle norme fixée arbitrairement. Le critère de la majorité claire ne pourra être jugé qu'après que le vote aura eu lieu et sera évalué en fonction de la qualité et de la transparence de la démarche ayant conduit au scrutin." Editorial, "Soyons clairs": *Le Devoir* (21 August 1998). For other editorials and points of view of interest, see "Éloge de la clarté": Alain Dubuc, *La Presse* (26 August 1998); "Le devoir de clarté": Bernard Descôteaux, *Le Devoir* (31 August 1998); "A 'Convincing' Majority": Julius Grey, *The Gazette* (5 September 1998).

[28] See, for example, the scholarly analysis of the *Quebec Secession Reference* by more than twenty constitutional lawyers, political scientists, and other experts contained in Daniel Drache and Patrick Monahan, eds., *Canada Watch*, Special Double Issue on the Reference, January–February 1999, Vol. 7, nos. 1–2 (a publication of the York University Centre for Public Law and Public Policy and the Robarts Centre for Canadian Studies).

[29] Pierre Bourgault, "Le testament": *Le Journal de Montréal* (23 August 1998).

Plusieurs sont surpris de m'entendre dire ça, mais c'est ce que je pense: la Cour a beaucoup de mérite d'avoir rendu un jugement aussi équilibré. La Cour écarte les perspectives de violence et d'extremisme, et c'est le rôle éminemment respectable que peut jouer une cour de justice. Il y a quelque chose d'apaisant, de sécurisant dans ce jugement par cette obligation qui est faite de négocier.[30]

It is to the wisdom of the Court's Reference opinion that this book now turns.

The Wisdom of the Reference Opinion

The opinion of the Supreme Court of Canada in the *Quebec Secession Reference* is one of those comparatively rare judgments that reflects the view of all nine judges of the Court, contains no dissenting opinions, and is rendered in the name of "THE COURT" itself, rather than, as in the case with other unanimous judgments, by one of the Justices writing on behalf of the other members of the Court.[31]

---

[30] "Les experts réagissent de façon positive": *La Presse* (21 August 1998).

[31] The Court has, it would seem, sought to reach a consensus for rendering *Coram* judgments in especially sensitive cases affecting Canada's Constitution, the country's territorial sovereignty, its national institutions, and its linguistic duality; at least half of these cases have involved issues concerning laws and policies of the legislature and government of Quebec and their relationship to constitutionally protected language rights or fundamental freedoms. Unanimous reasons for judgment written by "the Court" appear to begin with *Reference re Offshore Mineral Rights of British Columbia*, [1967] S.C.R. 792, affirming Canada's jurisdiction over the territorial seabed and continental shelf adjacent to British Columbia. Other *Coram* judgments include: *Attorney General of Quebec v. Blaikie*, [1979] 2 S.C.R. 1016 (affirming the decisions of the Superior Court and Court of Appeal striking down provisions of Quebec's *Charter of the French language* making French the only official language of the laws, legislature, and courts of the province, as contrary to s. 133 of the *Constitution Act, 1867*); *A.G. Manitoba v. Forest*, [1979] 2 S.C.R. 1032 (confirming the unconstitutionality of Manitoba's 1890 legislation making English the only official language of the laws, legislature, and courts of that province, as contrary to s. 23 of the *Manitoba Act, 1870*); *Reference re Authority of Parliament in relation to the Upper House*, [1980] 1 S.C.R. 54 (holding that the federal government's proposed legislation to reform the Senate would be *ultra vires*); *A.G. Quebec v. Blaikie (No 2)*, [1981] 1 S.C.R. 312 (confirming the extent to which the Court's earlier ruling applied to certain forms of delegated legislation); *Re Objection by Quebec to Resolution to Amend the Constitution*, [1982] 2 S.C.R. 793 (affirming the Quebec Court of Appeal's opinion that there was no constitutional convention recognizing a power of veto for the Government of Quebec over the patriation of the Constitution); *Reference re Newfoundland Continental Shelf*, [1984] 1 S.C.R. 86 (affirming Canada's jurisdiction over the mineral and natural resources of the seabed and subsoil of the continental shelf in the area offshore Newfoundland); *A.G. Quebec v. Quebec Association of Protestant School Boards*, [1984] 2 S.C.R. 66 (affirming the decisions of the Superior Court and Court of Appeal of Quebec that certain provisions of the *Charter of the French language* limiting access to education in English in the province were inconsistent with s. 23 of the *Canadian Charter of Rights and Freedoms*); *Reference re Manitoba Language Rights*, [1985] 1 S.C.R. 721 (holding all of Manitoba's unilingual laws since 1890 to be invalid and of no force and effect as contrary to s. 23 of the *Manitoba Act, 1870*, and preserving their operation for the minimum period necessary for re-enactment in English and French); *Ford v. Quebec*, [1988] 2 S.C.R. 712, and *Devine v. Quebec*, [1988] 2 S.C.R. 790 (holding that provisions of the *Charter of the French language* requiring public signs, posters, commercial advertising, and firm names to be solely in French infringed freedom of expression protected by both the Quebec and the Canadian Charters of Rights);

Those who were expecting a split in the Reference opinion between the judges on the Court from Quebec and the rest of Canada, or between English-speaking judges and French-speaking judges—a split that would magnify the cleavages that have appeared from time to time in our country over issues of national unity and identity, including the place of Quebec's role in the Canadian federation—were left without an issue to exploit. The Justices of the Supreme Court of Canada demonstrated discipline, cohesiveness, and no doubt an internal willingness to discuss, to seek compromise, and to subordinate strongly held individual views to the greater good of the whole.[32] This is both a reflection of the judges' profound sense of the importance of the questions before them in the Reference, and of their duty to respond to those questions in the clearest and most coherent manner possible in the circumstances of the case. Not only did the Justices of the Supreme Court bring much-needed clarity to the basic legal rules themselves, and to the debate about the proper place of those rules in regard to the secession process; they succeeded in doing so with elegance, sensitivity, reason, and logic that speak to the authority and the influence the Court justly commands as Canada's supreme judicial body, and to the Court's maturity, its confidence, and its institutional resilience in the face of sometimes scurrilous and un-warranted attacks by certain political actors during the course of the Reference.

The sagacity—the brilliance, even—of the Supreme Court of Canada's judgment in the *Quebec Secession Reference* lies in the Court's having had the vision to wed the value of constitutional legality with that of political legitimacy, and this on several levels.

The federal government and the Attorney General of Canada made the Reference to the Supreme Court to obtain clarity on the basic *legal* issues relating to the Quebec government's claim to be able to effect secession unilaterally, through the democratic principle and with the sanction of inter-national law. The sovereigntist leadership opposed the making of the Ref-erence because it had the potential to undermine the Government of Quebec's

---

Reference Re Manitoba Language Rights, [1992] 1 S.C.R. 212 (holding that s. 23 of the *Manitoba Act, 1870* applies to instruments of a legislative nature and to certain documents incorporated by reference into legislation); *Sinclair v. Quebec (A.G.)*, [1992] 1 S.C.R. 579 (striking down a series of legislative instruments because they did not meet the language requirements of s. 133 of the *Constitution Act, 1867*); and *Libman v. Quebec (A.G.)*, [1997] 3 S.C.R. 569 (invalidating certain provisions of Quebec's *Referendum Act* as infringing the guarantees of freedom of expression and association under the Quebec and Canadian Charters).

[32] "It's obviously the most important case the courts have been seized with because it goes to the very existence of the composition of our country. [...] Certainly none of us take this matter lightly." Chief Justice Antonio Lamer, quoted in "Top Court Gets Supreme Case": *Toronto Star* (16 February 1998); "La cause la plus importante de la carrière du juge en chef Lamer": *La Presse* (16 February 1998). "There were times when people had different points of view that hadn't been reconciled. [...] You keep going around the table and around the table. [...] There was some interest in the Court that everybody should be able to read it. It wasn't written for the law professors and lawyers alone. It's a document of great interest to most Canadians, and it should be something that most of them can read if they choose to read it. [...] I think it will stand the test of time. That's what we were trying to do: produce something that will stand that test." Mr. Justice John Major, quoted in: "Behind the Scenes as History Was Made": Sean Finn, *Globe & Mail* (21 August 1998).

claim to have the legal capacity to act without any regard to the constitutional law of Canada, and would subject that claim to the so-called "straitjacket" of the Canadian Constitution and its amendment procedures.

The Supreme Court of Canada has confirmed that unilateral secession would be an unlawful act under the Constitution and a violation of the Canadian legal order; a revolution. Nor is there any legal right at international law, whether as a matter of self-determination or otherwise, to unilateral secession in the circumstances of Quebec. Secession, to be lawful under the Constitution of Canada, would require a constitutional amendment.

At the same time, the Court recognized that the sovereigntist movement in Quebec would obtain democratic legitimacy for the secessionist option if a clear majority of Quebecers, on a clear question, expressed their desire to leave Canada. Moreover, that clear expression of desire would trigger an obligation on all parties to the federation to negotiate the terms and conditions of secession.

This, of course, was an interesting and unexpected surprise for the sovereigntists, many if not all of whose spokespersons, as we have seen, immediately embraced this aspect of the Court's ruling. The Government of Quebec's Minister of Intergovernmental Affairs, Jacques Brassard, was the first to warm to the judgment of the Court. Deputy Premier Bernard Landry soon followed suit. Even former Premier Parizeau discovered common ground with the Supreme Court, stating that the threat of a U.D.I. had only been a lever for negotiations, which the Court had now guaranteed.[33] Premier Bouchard, who had campaigned relentlessly against the Supreme Court and the Reference, especially on the eve of the hearing in February, suddenly switched gears; the Supreme Court's decision was no less than one of the "winning conditions" for the next sovereignty referendum. No longer, said the sovereigntist leadership, could the federal government deny the legitimacy of the sovereigntist option, or that there would be negotiations following a majority YES vote.

However, what is capital to remember is that the democratic principle that would legitimize the sovereigntist option is characterized by the Court as an inherent principle of the *Constitution of Canada*. The obligation to negotiate is a *constitutional* duty, flowing both from the *constitutional* principle of democracy and the right and responsibility of democratically elected representatives to initiate *constitutional amendments* under Part V of the *Constitution Act, 1982*. The secession of a province legally requires an *amendment* to the *Constitution*, which perforce requires negotiation.

Moreover, the duty to negotiate is a *reciprocal* obligation on all parties, the corollary of a legitimate attempt by one participant in Confederation *to seek an amendment to the Constitution*. The *conduct* of the parties would be governed by *constitutional* principles: federalism, democracy, *constitutionalism itself* and the rule of law, and the protection of minorities. There

---

[33] "Parizeau considère sa démarche réhabilitée": *Le Devoir,* (22 August 1998); "Threat of Unilateral Declaration Was Always Meant to Force Negotiation, Parizeau Says": *Globe & Mail* (21 August 1998).

would be *no legal obligation* on the other provinces and federal government to give effect to an act of secession in the Constitution; "that would not be a negotiation at all." The democratic principle could not be invoked to trump the principles of federalism and the rule of law, the rights of individuals and minorities, or the operation of democracy in the other provinces or in Canada as a whole; but at the same time, the *Canadian constitutional order* could not remain indifferent to the clear expression of a clear majority of Quebecers that they no longer wish to remain in Canada. Otherwise, this would mean that the other *constitutional* principles necessarily trump the clearly expressed democratic will of Quebecers. That would give insufficient weight to the underlying principles that *must inform the amendment process.* None of the rights or principles is absolute to the exclusion of the others.

The negotiations would have to address the interests of the federal government, Quebec, the other provinces, other participants, as well as the rights of all Canadians both within and outside Quebec, and would require the reconciliation of the various rights and obligations by the representatives of *two legitimate majorities*, the clear majority of the population of Quebec, and the clear majority of Canada as a whole. A political majority that did not act in accordance with the underlying *constitutional* principles would put at risk the *legitimacy* of the exercise of its rights. The *conduct* of the parties would assume primary *constitutional* significance. Secession could not be achieved under the *Constitution* unilaterally; that is, without *principled* negotiation *within* the *existing constitutional framework.*

What all this amounts to is that **sovereigntists as much as federalists have a stake in the proper operation and application of the Constitution of Canada.** The Constitution, including its underlying principles, its rights and obligations, and its amendment procedures, is relevant for sovereigntists (whether or not they fully realize or admit it), because it safeguards their legitimate interests, just as it does those of all Canadians.

This finding of the Court is immensely salutary for Canada's civic traditions and political culture. It is not healthy for a substantial portion of the country's population to perceive, rightly or wrongly, that its interests are perpetually "outside" the structure of the country's supreme and fundamental law, anymore than it is healthy for a provincial government to act as if it can ignore the law. The Supreme Court judgment welcomes them back into the fold. There are no "enemies of the State" in Canada when it comes to advancing a political cause, even one as extraordinary as secession, so long as that cause and those who propound it respect the legal framework and basic constitutional values that govern the making of political choices in a free and democratic society like ours.

But in embracing the Court's finding of an obligation to negotiate, sovereigntists must also accept the Court's rules as to the circumstances in which such a duty would arise—a clear expression of a clear majority of a desire to secede from Canada—and the rules governing the conduct of the negotiations: respect by *all* participants, including the sovereigntist government, of the underlying principles of the Constitution of Canada identified by the Court as applicable to the secession context. This includes respect for the principle of the rule of law, but also of *constitutionalism*, which the Court went out of its way to particularize as being embodied in s. 52(1) of the *Constitution Act, 1982* and requiring that all government action comply with the Constitution.

Subsection 52(1) provides that the Constitution of Canada is the "supreme law" of the country, and that "any law that is inconsistent with the provisions of the Constitution is [...] of no force or effect." As the Court stated in para. 72 of its opinion: "The Constitution binds all governments, both federal and provincial, including the executive branch. [...] They may not transgress its provisions: indeed, their sole claim to exercise lawful authority rests in the powers allotted to them under the Constitution, and can come from no other source."

Respect for *constitutionalism*—especially in circumstances such as secession, where a constitutional amendment is required and where a duty to negotiate arises as a corollary to the right to initiate constitutional change under the *Constitution Act, 1982*—must mean, at least, respect for the provisions that govern the procedure for amending the Constitution.

The Court's balanced decision provides all participants in the Canadian federation with a chance to pause, and perhaps to conduct the debate over the future of Canada and Quebec with a vocabulary that is less absolutist, less strident in rhetoric and tone, more respectful of the other side's traditions, institutions, values, hopes, and aspirations, as well as more mindful of the degree to which many of those values and aspirations are mutually shared and flow from a common history together.

The Legal Effect of the Reference Opinion

The Supreme Court of Canada's judgment in the *Quebec Secession Reference* was given by the Court in its advisory, rather than its adjudicative, capacity. It does not result in a disposition of rights in the way a judgment rendered in an appeal would, in the context of litigation. Only in the *Manitoba Language Rights Reference* did the Court issue a binding declaration, and that was due to the need to preserve the constitutional principle of the rule of law in the extraordinary circumstances of that case.

This is not to ignore or to gainsay the compelling nature of a reference decision and its effect on our legal system. Some of the most important rulings of the Supreme Court in the area of constitutional law have been made in the context of references—the *Senate Reference*, the *Patriation Reference*, the *Quebec Veto Reference*, the *Manitoba Language Rights Reference* itself, *Reference re Public Schools Act (Manitoba)*, and the *Provincial Judges Reference*—to mention a few of the more recent ones. Reference opinions have always been treated as binding by our courts, legislatures, and governments.[34] They are legal pronouncements of the highest court in the land.

---

[34] See, e.g., Peter W. Hogg, *Constitutional Law of Canada*, 4th ed. (Toronto: Carswell, 1997), 8.6 (d). "In practice, reference opinions are treated in the same way as other judicial

In his comments following the release of the Supreme Court's decision in the *Quebec Secession Reference*, Quebec's Minister of Intergovernmental Affairs, Jacques Brassard, declared the Court's opinion to be a "simple avis," not a judgment binding on the Government of Quebec. How, then, he was asked by journalists, could he insist on the Court's finding that the duty to negotiate secession would be, as the Court had stated, a binding obligation? And if the obligation, which the Court had characterized as reciprocal, was not binding on the Government of Quebec because it was a "simple avis," why would it bind the Government of Canada? Mr. Brassard was forced by his own logic into a rather embarrassing position:

> Est-ce que le fédéral va juger qu'il est contraint de s'asseoir à une table de négociation? Ma réponse, c'est non, puisqu'il faut bien que je sois cohérent.[35]

However, the day after the ruling, Premier Bouchard was categorical about the obligation to negotiate imposed by the Court:

> Les juges fédéraux affirment et répètent qu'après un Oui, le Canada aura l'obligation de négocier avec le Québec. Ils en font même obligation constitutionelle. [...]
>
> À elle seule, l'obligation faite au Canada de négocier avec le Québec dissipe l'incertitude que faisait peser dans l'esprit de beaucoup de Québécois le refus de négocier des fédéralistes. Ces Québécois se trouvent aujourd'hui rassurés: leur Oui forcera le Canada à négocier.[36]

As *Le Devoir* editorialized in regard to Mr. Bouchard's statement:

> Il est assez paradoxal de voir M. Bouchard célébrer aujourd'hui le contenu d'un jugement dont il ne reconnaît pourtant pas la valeur juridique. [...] [L]e président du Parti québécois ne peut pas prendre dans l'avis de la cour ce qui lui plaît et rejeter ce qui ne l'intéresse pas. Ainsi, pour que cette obligation de négocier soit valable, le résultat du référendum doit être sans ambiguités, écrivent les juges avec insistance.[37]

The better view was later taken by counsel for Mr. Bouchard and for the Attorney General of Quebec, Mr. Serge Ménard, before the Court of Appeal

---

opinions." There is one case where a judge called into question the Supreme Court's ability, in the *Manitoba Language Rights Reference*, to make a binding declaration of invalidity of Manitoba's unilingual laws and yet also to preserve their continued operation for the period of time required for re-enactment in both English and French. In *Yeryk v. Yeryk*, [1985] 5 W.W.R. 705 at p. 710 *et seq.*, O'Sullivan J.A. of the Manitoba Court of Appeal stated: "I do not understand how a court would put pressure on the Queen in that way. [...] I do not understand how the Supreme Court or any other court has a power to declare judicially valid or enforceable that which is judicially invalid. I do not understand how it can be said that emergency situations justify a usurpation by the Court of the royal power. [...] The Supreme Court cannot dictate to the Queen in right of Manitoba." Chief Justice Monnin stated (at p. 709) that his colleague's comments were "gratuitous, unnecessary, injudicious and perhaps impertinent. I disassociate myself entirely from them."

[35] Press Conference of Minister Brassard (20 August 1998); *La Presse* (21 August 1998).

[36] Premier Bouchard's statement (21 August 1998), *supra*.

[37] "Soyons clairs," Michel Venne, editorial, *Le Devoir* (22 August 1998).

of Quebec in the second *Bertrand* case, *Bertrand v. Bouchard et autres (Bertrand (N° 2))*.[38] In his factum, the Attorney General of Quebec (on his own behalf and on behalf of the Premier),

> tient à souligner [...] que le 20 août 1998, la Cour suprême du Canada a rendu un avis concernant la légalité d'une éventuelle déclaration unilatérale de souveraineté du Québec (*Renvoi relatif à la sécession du Québec* [...])[39]

The Attorney General of Quebec went on to argue in the factum that the issues raised by Mr. Bertrand in his proceedings, insofar as they relate to

> une déclaration de souveraineté du Québec faite:
>
> • de façon unilatérale
>
> • en contravention avec la constitution canadienne; et/ou
>
> • sans acceptation de la part du gouvernement fédéral [...]
>
> ont déjà fait l'objet de l'avis de la Cour suprême dans le Renvoi sur la sécession du Québec prononcé le 20 août 1998.[40]

The Attorney General of Quebec also recognized that in the proceedings in *Bertrand (N° 1)* before Justices Lesage and Pidgeon, respectively, Mr. Bertrand "demandait à la Cour de déclarer inconstitutionnel le projet de sécession unilatérale du Québec alors que cette question a maintenant fait l'objet d'avis de la Cour suprême du Canada." The Attorney General of Quebec then cited the Supreme Court's pronouncement in para. 105 of its opinion that "we refrain from pronouncing on the applicability of any particular constitutional procedure to effect secession *unless and until sufficiently clear facts exist to squarely raise an issue for judicial determination*," and in para. 139 to the effect that concerns "precipitated by the *asserted right of Quebec to unilateral secession*" need not be explored further, "*[i]n*

---

[38] *Bertrand c. Bouchard*, [1998] R.J.Q. 1203 (Sup. Ct. of Quebec, *per* Blanchard J.) The plaintiff sought a declaratory judgment to the effect that should the Government of Quebec proceed with a unilateral declaration of independence, he would be entitled to pay his provincial taxes into an administrative trust and to continue to pay his federal taxes to the federal government. The Attorney General of Quebec filed a motion to dismiss the case as hypothetical because there was no imminence of another referendum, and premature because it presupposed the result of the Reference then pending before the Supreme Court of Canada on the issue of the legality of Quebec's secessionist project. The Attorney General of Canada, who was *mise en cause* in this case, argued that proceedings in the case should be adjourned until after the hearing and judgment in the *Quebec Secession Reference*. (I disclose that I was co-counsel for the Attorney General of Canada in this matter.) Mr. Justice Jacques Blanchard, in a judgment rendered on March 6, 1998, dismissed the case as hypothetical and premature, given the absence of an imminent referendum and given the pending Reference, respectively. The plaintiff appealed the dismissal of his case to the Court of Appeal of Quebec, and the appeal was to be heard on September 16, 1999 (C.A. 200-09-001975-983). However, in August 1999, the plaintiff desisted and withdrew his appeal, with the consent of all parties.

[39] Factum of the Attorney General of Quebec on behalf of the respondents Bouchard and Ménard, filed with the Court of Appeal of Quebec on September 23, 1998; para. 6.

[40] Factum of the Attorney General of Quebec, paras. 23 and 24.

*light of our finding that there is no such right applicable to the population
of Quebec*, either under the Constitution of Canada or at international law."[41]

In other words, the Attorney General of Quebec has invoked the opinion
of the Supreme Court of Canada in the *Quebec Secession Reference* and
the Court's finding that there is no right to unilateral secession—in a case
before the courts of Quebec. I mention this not to express agreement or
disagreement in any way with the Attorney General of Quebec's position
on the appeal or on the merits of Mr. Bertrand's case, but simply to illustrate
that the Attorney General of Quebec has clearly accepted—as the Attorney
General must, in fact—that the Supreme Court of Canada's opinion in the
Quebec Secession Reference is now an important part of the relevant constitutional jurisprudence that applies in the Canadian legal system, including
the courts of Quebec.

There should be nothing remarkable in this, had it not been for the
extraordinary position taken by the Government and the Attorney General
of Quebec *before* the *Quebec Secession Reference*, to the effect that the
Canadian Constitution and the courts have no role to play in respect of the
legality of the Government of Quebec's proposed secession process. It is
clear that in a proper case, giving rise to justiciable issues within a concrete
set of facts, the Supreme Court's opinion in the *Quebec Secession Reference*
could have a role to play. As the Chief Justice of the Supreme Court stated
in the *Provincial Judges Reference*, "the fact that this Court's opinion is
only advisory does not leave the parties without a remedy. They can seek a
declaration [from the superior court of the province], and this Court's opinion
will be of highly persuasive weight."[42]

Evidently, in the context of the *Quebec Secession Reference*, what would
be a proper case will turn on whether the issues are legal and justiciable,
and whether the courts have an appropriate role in their disposition.

For example, within days of the release of the Supreme Court's opinion
in the *Quebec Secession Reference*, the Trial Division of the Federal Court
was seized with an application[43] by members of the Reform Party for an
interlocutory injunction to restrain the Governor General of Canada from
appointing to the Senate a qualified person from the Province of Alberta,
unless that person had been "elected" pursuant to the provisions of Alberta's
Senatorial Selection Act. The principle of democracy and the Supreme Court's
opinion in the *Quebec Secession Reference* were heavily relied upon by the
applicants. The Attorney General of Canada argued that the provisions of
the *Constitution Act, 1867* expressly confer on the Governor General the
unfettered discretion to appoint qualified persons to the Senate. Madam
Justice McGillis dismissed the application, noting *inter alia* that "nothing

---

[41] Factum of the Attorney General of Quebec, para. 116; the italicized words were underlined by counsel for the Attorney General of Quebec, quoting the French version of paras.
105 and 139 of the opinion of the Supreme Court in the Reference.

[42] *Reference re Provincial Court Judges, supra*, reasons for judgment on rehearing reported at [1998] 1 S.C.R. 3; at para. 10.

[43] *Samson et al. v. Attorney General of Canada et al.* (Fed. Ct. T.D., docket T-1706-98).

in that case [the *Quebec Secession Reference*] supports the proposition th;
a court may ignore the express and unequivocal provisions of the *Constitution Act, 1867*."[44]

The *Quebec Secession Reference* was also invoked by the plaintiffs in
*Hogan et al. v. Attorney General of Newfoundland and Attorney General of
Canada*,[45] a challenge to the validity of the *Constitution Amendment, 1998
(Newfoundland Act)*. The plaintiffs claimed that the amendment in relation
to Term 17 of the Terms of Union of Newfoundland with Canada dealing
with denominational rights in the province violated the principle of the
protection of minority rights and the rule of law, notably due to alleged
unfairness in the conduct of the provincial government's referendum on the
proposed amendment, and because the rights in issue could only be amended
under the general amending formula of the Constitution.

The Attorney General of Canada argued, *inter alia*, that this amendment
had been lawfully enacted under the procedure set out in s. 43 of the
Constitution Act, 1982, which provides that an amendment in relation to a
provision of the Constitution of Canada that applies to one or more but not
all provinces may be made only with the consent of the Senate, the House
of Commons, and the legislative assembly of the province to which the
amendment applies. Term 17, it was argued, is a provision that applies only
to one province, and the amendment had been approved by the House of
Assembly of the province and by the federal houses. The referendum did
not affect the validity of the constitutional amendment because it was not a
part of the procedures set out in *Part V* of the *Constitution Act, 1982*. Mr.
Justice Riche of the Supreme Court of Newfoundland dismissed the challenge
to the validity of the amendment and cited the Supreme Court of Canada in
the *Quebec Secession Reference* for his finding that the referendum "does
not play a *legal role* in constitutional amendment" and that "[l]egally the
referendum is not part of the amending procedure."[46]

---

[44] *Ibid.* Reasons for order of McGillis J., delivered from the Bench on September 1, 1998;
para. 7; now reported at (1998) 165 D.L.R. (4th) 342; see also the memorandum of judgment
of the Court of Appeal of Alberta in *Bert Brown v. The Queen et al.* filed on August 31, 1999
(docket 17949), wherein the Court of Appeal states (at para. 25): "We agree with the Crown
that the appellant 'seeks to invoke the democratic principle, *per se*, divorced of its interpre-
tive role and devoid of legal issues, simply because a declaratory order from the Court would,
in his view, "have considerable persuasive effect, and it would confer democratic legitimacy
on the *Senatorial Selection Act*."' We do not view the Supreme Court's statements in the
Quebec Secession Reference as modifying the existing jurisprudence on what constitutes a
legal issue."

[45] Supreme Court of Newfoundland, Trial Division; docket: 1997 St. J. No. 2526. I disclose
that I was counsel for the Attorney General of Canada in this matter.

[46] *Ibid.* Decision of Riche J., filed January 14, 1999; paras. 26–28; emphasis in original;
now reported at (1999), 173 Nfld. & P.E.I.R. 148, 530 A.P.R. 148. This decision has been
appealed to the Court of Appeal; the appeal was heard on June 14 to 17, 1999; judgment is
pending. Some similar issues are raised in the appeal from the decision of Côté J. of the
Quebec Superior Court in *Potter et al. v. A.G. Quebec and A.G. Canada*, [1999] R.J.Q. 165.
(I disclose that I am counsel for the Attorney General of Canada in both appeals.) A hearing
date has not yet been set in the *Potter* appeal.

16

ses serve to illustrate that the courts will be guided by the
urt's judicial opinion in the *Quebec Secession Reference* and
t to the extent the particular circumstances of the case before
warrant, just as they do with other decisions of the Supreme
Court of Canada.

In the secession context, circumstances might arise at some point that
might require further judicial consideration and clarification. The Supreme
Court itself has pointed to the amending procedure for effecting the secession of a province as being one of the legal issues that might be dealt with
judicially, if a sufficient set of concrete facts were to give rise to a justiciable
issue. "Secession is a legal act as much as a political one."

The Court will exercise no supervisory role over "political issues that
lack a legal component" and the "political aspects of constitutional negotiations"; these are left by the Court, and properly so, to the political actors
to evaluate, assess, and resolve. However, the Court adds, "[t]his does not
deprive the surrounding constitutional framework of its binding status, nor
does this mean that constitutional obligations could be breached without
incurring serious legal repercussions." This is certainly a message that
suggests that governments would do well to consider themselves bound by
this ruling, even if, formally, it is an advisory opinion and not a declaratory
judgment.

This message was acknowledged in the statement of the Minister of
Justice and Attorney General of Canada, the Honourable Anne McLellan,
after the Supreme Court released its decision. The opinion of the Court,
she stated, "shows wisdom" and "merits the respect of all Canadians."

> It has produced a balanced and carefully considered decision. The
> Government of Canada will respect and follow its opinion. We expect
> that all governments and citizens of Canada will do the same.

How Far We Have Come: Key Findings of the Court

Until the Government of Canada began to challenge the myths and assump-
tions of the sovereigntist position on the legal questions relating to the
secession of Quebec from Canada, the position of the Government of Quebec
on this issue could be fairly summarized as follows:

• that a simple majority vote in a referendum in the province, on a
question formulated by the Government of Quebec, would give that government not only the democratic mandate but also the legal authority to effect
the secession of Quebec from Canada unilaterally;

• that the Government of Quebec's "process of accession to sovereignty,"
by which Quebec would no longer be a province of Canada, but rather an
independent state, is a process that operates wholly outside of and without
reference to the Canadian constitutional framework;

• that the Constitution of Canada is irrelevant to that process;

• that a constitutional amendment would not be required to effect the
secession of Quebec lawfully;

- that the courts of Canada and Quebec, including the Superior Court of Quebec, have no jurisdiction over any aspect of the matter;

- that it is within the legislative competence of the National Assembly, legislature, and government of Quebec to enact laws or to proclaim measures such as the Draft Bill, *An Act respecting the sovereignty of Québec*, and Bill 1, *An Act respecting the future of Québec*, which would purport to authorize, enforce, and make binding a unilateral declaration of independence;

- that the authority of those legislative and governmental bodies to effect Quebec's secession flows from the role of those bodies as democratic institutions and instruments of the sovereign will of the people;

- that this process of unilateral secession is sanctioned by international law, including the international right of peoples to self-determination;

- that Canada's territorial integrity as a sovereign state has no bearing on the issue;

- that Canadians have no say or right of participation in a matter of this nature affecting the future of their country;

- that negotiations between Canada and Quebec would be negotiations with a view to establishing a partnership treaty between two sovereign states;

- that the National Assembly of Quebec would control the timing and the terms of those negotiations, which in principle would last one year from the date of a majority YES vote in a referendum; in the event of a failure in the negotiations, the National Assembly would be empowered to proclaim Quebec's independence unilaterally;

- that secession is exclusively a political, not a legal, matter.

What the Supreme Court of Canada's opinion in the *Quebec Secession Reference* has clarified and confirmed are at least the following points:

- The *Constitution Act, 1982* is in force and its legality is unassailable.[47]

- The existence and application of constitutional principles cannot be taken as a invitation to dispense with the written text of the Constitution; there are compelling reasons to insist upon the primacy of the written Constitution, including the promotion of legal certainty and predictability.[48]

- Secession is a legal act as much as a political one.[49]

- The legality of unilateral secession must be evaluated, at least in the first instance, from the perspective of the domestic legal order of the state from which the unit seeks to withdraw.[50]

---

[47] Para. 32.

[48] Para. 53.

[49] Para. 83.

[50] Para. 83.

- The secession of a province must be considered, in legal terms, to require an amendment to the Constitution.[51]

- It lies within the power of the people of Canada, acting through their various governments, to effect the secession of Quebec from Canada.[52]

- The *Constitution Act, 1982* confers a right to initiate constitutional change on each participant in Confederation. The amendment of the Constitution begins with a political process undertaken pursuant to the Constitution itself.[53]

- The initiative for constitutional amendment is the responsibility of democratically elected participants in Confederation, the democratically elected representatives of the people.[54]

- The Constitution does not address the use of a referendum procedure, and the results of a referendum have no direct role or legal effect in our constitutional scheme, although democratically elected representatives may, of course, take their cue from a referendum.[55]

- The secession of Quebec from Canada cannot by accomplished by the National Assembly, the legislature, or the government of Quebec unilaterally, i.e., without principled negotiations, and be considered a lawful act.[56]

- Any attempt to effect the secession of a province from Canada must be undertaken pursuant to the Constitution of Canada, or else violate the Canadian legal order.[57]

- The National Assembly, legislature, and government of Quebec are institutions that clearly exist as part of the Canadian legal order.[58]

- The Constitution binds all governments, both federal and provincial; they may not transgress its provisions; their sole claim to exercise lawful authority rests in the powers allocated to them under the Constitution and can come from no other source.[59]

- Acceptance of a principle of effectivity would be tantamount to accepting that the National Assembly, legislature, or government of Quebec may act without regard to the law, simply because it asserts the power to do so. The suggestion that the National Assembly, legislature, or government of Quebec could purport to secede the province unilaterally from Canada in disregard of Canadian and international law, by means of an unconstitutional

---

[51] Para. 84.

[52] Para. 85.

[53] Paras. 69 and 88.

[54] Para. 88.

[55] Paras. 87 and 88.

[56] Para. 104.

[57] Para. 104.

[58] Para. 23.

[59] Para. 72.

declaration of secession leading to a *de facto* secession, is an assertion of fact, not a statement of law; it may or may not be true. If it is put forward as an assertion of law, then it amounts to the contention that the law may be broken as long as it can be broken successfully. Such a notion is contrary to the rule of law and must be rejected.[60]

• Lawful secession requires a constitutional amendment, and a constitutional amendment perforce requires negotiation.[61]

• The constitutional principle of democracy would require that considerable weight be given to a clear expression by the people of Quebec of their will to secede from Canada, even though a referendum, in and of itself and without more, has no direct legal effect, and could not bring about unilateral secession.[62]

• The referendum result, if it is to be taken as an expression of the democratic will, must be free of ambiguity, both in terms of the question asked and in terms of the support it achieves.[63]

• Such an expression of democratic will would confer legitimacy on the efforts of the Government of Quebec to initiate the Constitution's amendment process in order to secede by constitutional means.[64]

• The corollary of a legitimate attempt by one participant in Confederation to seek an amendment to the Constitution is an obligation on all parties to come to the negotiating table.[65]

• The conduct of the parties in such negotiations would be governed by the same constitutional principles that give rise to the duty to negotiate: federalism, democracy, constitutionalism and the rule of law, and the protection of minorities.[66]

• There is no legal obligation on the other provinces and the federal government to accede to the secession of a province, subject only to negotiation of the logistical details of secession. Quebec could not purport to invoke a right of self-determination such as to dictate the terms of a proposed secession to the other parties: that would not be a negotiation at all. The democracy principle cannot be invoked to trump the principles of federalism and the rule of law, the rights of individuals and minorities, or the operation of democracy in the other provinces or in Canada as a whole. No negotiations could be effective if their ultimate outcome, secession, is cast as an absolute legal entitlement to give effect to that secession in the Constitution.[67]

---

[60] Paras 106, 107, and 108.

[61] Para. 84.

[62] Para. 87.

[63] Para. 87.

[64] Para. 87.

[65] Para. 88.

[66] Para. 90.

[67] Paras. 90 and 91.

- However, the continued existence and operation of the Canadian constitutional order could not remain indifferent to the clear expression of a clear majority of Quebecers that they no longer wish to remain in Canada. This would amount to the assertion that other constitutionally recognized principles trump the clearly expressed democratic will of the people of Quebec. The rights of other provinces and the federal government cannot deny the right of the government of Quebec to pursue secession, should a clear majority of the people of Quebec choose that goal, so long as in doing so, Quebec respects the rights of others.[68]

- Refusal of a party to conduct negotiations in a manner consistent with constitutional principles would seriously put at risk the legitimacy of that party's assertion of its rights.[69]

- No one can predict the course that such negotiations might take. Negotiations would inevitably address a wide range of important issues, including national economic interests, the national debt, boundary issues, linguistic and cultural minorities, aboriginal peoples, and many other issues of great complexity and difficulty, which would have to be resolved within the overall framework of the rule of law.[70]

- As for international law, it contains neither a right of unilateral secession nor the explicit denial of such a right, although such a denial is implicit in the exceptional circumstances required for secession to be permitted under the right of a people to self-determination.[71]

- International law places great importance on the territorial integrity of national states, and, by and large, leaves the creation of a new state to be determined by the domestic law of the existing state of which the seceding entity presently forms a part.[72]

- International law expects that the right to self-determination will be exercised by peoples within the framework of existing sovereign states and consistently with the maintenance of the territorial integrity of those states.[73]

- While much of the Quebec population certainly shares many of the characteristics (such as a common language and culture) that would be considered in determining whether a specific group is a "people" within the meaning of the exercise of the international law right of self-determination, it is not necessary to explore this legal characterization further, because the right of self-determination cannot in present circumstances ground a right to unilateral secession.[74]

---

[68] Para. 92.

[69] Para. 95.

[70] Para. 96.

[71] Para. 112.

[72] Para. 112.

[73] Para. 122.

[74] Para. 125.

• The international law right to self-determination only generates, at best, a right to external self-determination in situations of former colonies; where a people is oppressed, as for example under a foreign military occupation; or where a definable group is denied meaningful access to government to pursue their political, economic, social, and cultural development. Such exceptional circumstances are manifestly inapplicable to Quebec under existing conditions.[75]

• Accordingly, neither the population of the province of Quebec nor its representative institutions, the National Assembly, the legislature, or the government of Quebec, possess a right, under international law, to secede unilaterally from Canada.[76]

• It may be that a unilateral secession by Quebec would eventually be accorded legal status by Canada and other states, and thus give rise to legal consequences; but this does not support the more radical contention that subsequent recognition of a state of affairs brought about by a unilateral declaration of independence could be taken to mean that secession was achieved under colour of a legal right.[77]

The Future

On November 30, 1998, the Parti Québécois government of Premier Lucien Bouchard was re-elected with a majority of seats in the National Assembly, but a smaller share of the popular vote than that obtained by the opposition Quebec Liberal Party.[78] Initially, Mr. Bouchard appeared to rule out another sovereignty referendum, at least in the near future, on the basis that it was clear from the vote that Quebecers do not want another referendum.

> Mise en veilleuse? Oui, je crois que les Québécois nous ont dit que le temps n'est pas propice à la tenue d'un référendum dans l'immédiat.
>
> La décision de lundi signifie très clairement que les Québécois n'estiment pas réunies les conditions d'un référendum gagnant. Les Québécois ne veulent pas de référendum actuellement, ça me parait évident. Qu'on finisse le travail que nous avons commencé. Ils veulent qu'on fasse progresser le Québec. Et c'est ce que nous allons faire. Je comprends très bien le message, je l'accepte et nous allons nous y conformer.
>
> On verra par la suite si les Québécois augmentent leur niveau de confiance en eux-mêmes, si cela pourra conduire à la création des conditions gagnantes qui permettront un référendum.[79]

---

[75] Para. 138.

[76] Para. 138.

[77] Para. 144.

[78] The Parti Québécois received 42.7% of the vote; the Quebec Liberal Party received 43.7%. Most of the rest of the vote went to the Action Démocratique du Québec.

[79] "L'option référendaire en veilleuse": *Le Devoir*; "La souveraineté va attendre": *Le Journal de Montréal*; "Pas de référendum, le message est clair, constate le premier ministre": *La Presse*; "Référendum en veilleuse": *Le Soleil*; "Bouchard Puts Off Referendum": *Globe & Mail* (2 December 1998).

Mr. Bouchard later affirmed, however, that his government had received a mandate to hold another referendum, once the "winning conditions" are established.

> Nous avons un mandat pour faire un référendum, c'est évident. Nous l'avons sollicité ce mandat, nous avons été assez clairs. Nous avons à réunir les conditions gagnantes.[80]

In his "Discours d'ouverture"—the equivalent of the Speech from the Throne—on March 3, 1999, Premier Bouchard formalized this commitment before the National Assembly of Quebec.

> L'ouverture d'un nouveau millénaire porte avec lui une attente et une ouverture d'esprit. Il y aura, demain et après demain, un moment—une année, peut-être—où nous pourrons, mieux que d'habitude, donner une impulsion, prendre les décisions essentielles pour l'avenir. [...]
>
> La souveraineté et le fédéralisme? Bien sûr nous en débattrons, chacun dans nos partis et ensemble. [...] Cependant, il est indubitable que la réunion des conditions d'un référendum gagnant sur la souveraineté fait partie du mandat que nous avons sollicité et obtenu. L'enjeu politique de l'élection était clair pour tout le monde.
>
> Pour le moment, les électeurs québécois se sont mis à peu de chose près au neutre. [...]
>
> Il ne faut pas se méprendre. Le peuple du Québec a démontré dans le passé une capacité de rebondissement considérable. Nous savons tous que cette capacité est toujours là, prête à se manifester. Mais nous devons être francs et dire aux Québécoises et aux Québécois que, dans le contexte canadien actuel, il y a un prix politique à payer pour rester trop longtemps dans l'indécision.[81]

The leader of the Opposition, Jean Charest, replied that the plurality of the popular vote received by his party contained a message to the effect that

> les Québécoises et les Québécois sont fatigués, épuisés, exaspérés par le débat stérile et sans issue que leur impose ce régime du Parti québécois sur leur avenir. L'obsession des péquistes, qui les mène à vouloir tenir des référendums à répétition, jusqu'à ce qu'ils aient arraché le résultat qu'ils souhaitent mais que la population a dit et redit qu'elle ne souhaite pas, cette obsession, dis-je, est devenue, pour les citoyens et citoyennes, un très lourd fardeau. En effet, M. Le Président, plus personne aujourd'hui ne peu nier le prix exorbitant que nous payons sur les plans économique, politique et social pour l'incertitude dans laquelle les gens d'en face s'acharnent à nous maintenir par tous les moyens depuis bientôt cinq ans. [...]
>
> Nos concitoyens, M. Le Président, ne veulent surtout pas un autre référendum à l'ordre du jour de l'Assemblée nationale dans le prochain

---

[80] "Un référendum après le mi-mandat": *Le Devoir*; "PQ Has Referendum Mandate: Bouchard": *The Gazette*; "Bouchard Holds Firm on Sovereignty Referendum": *Toronto Star* (8 December 1998).

[81] Discours inaugural du premier ministre du Québec, M. Lucien Bouchard, lors de l'ouverture de la 36ᵉ législature à l'Assemblée nationale, Québec, le 3 mars 1999; débats de l'Assemblée nationale.

mandat. Bien au contraire, ils souhaitent que leurs élus se penchent sur leurs problèmes, qui sont réels, qui sont criants. C'était tellement clair que, le soir de l'élection, que, le lendemain, le premier ministre du Québec, nouvellement élu, n'a pas pu éviter de constater qu'il n'avait pas le mandat de tenir un référendum. [...]

Or, ce gouvernement est coincé, d'autre part, par son option, par un parti politique dont l'engagement primordial, pour ne pas dire existentiel, est de réaliser la sécession du Québec. [...]

[T]he people of Québec have voted twice in a referendum that they want to pursue their future within Canada, Mr. Speaker. It was true in 1980, it was true in 1995, true in 1998 and true in 1999, Mr. Speaker.[82]

The debate thus continues, as it should, amongst the political actors and democratically elected representatives of Quebecers and Canadians. The Parti Québécois leadership has established a "comité de réflexion et d'actions stratégiques" presided by Minister Bernard Landry that will examine ways and means to package and to promote the sovereignty option, with a view to the next full-scale party convention in Montreal on May 5 to 7, 2000, which will be devoted to the sovereignty issue. The Bloc Québécois, for its part, has engaged Jacques Parizeau as the chair of a workshop on Quebec and its place in the world, one of four workshops whose reports will provide the backdrop to a number of regional fora on Quebec sovereignty leading up to the Bloc's own party convention in January 2000, in Quebec City. Mr. Jean Charest has appointed newly elected MNA Benoît Pelletier, formerly a professor of constitutional law at the University of Ottawa, to chair a Quebec Liberal Party committee, the task of which is to review and update the QLP's constitutional program, *Reconnaissance et Interdépendance—l'identité québécoise et le fédéralisme canadien*, which was produced by the Comité sur l'évolution du fédéralisme canadien of the QLP in December 1996.

There will be much room, then, for reflection and debate among Quebecers and, indeed, all Canadians, during the first year of the next century. As the Supreme Court of Canada stated in the *Quebec Secession Reference,* "a functioning democracy requires a continuous process of discussion." The Supreme Court's opinion in the Reference is well on its way to becoming, as one commentator has aptly described it,[83] a classic of contemporary constitutional law. That the debate on our future will take place with an additional degree of clarity, in circumstances of some serenity, and with a better understanding and appreciation of the legal framework within which fundamental political choices are made in this country, is in no small part due to the profoundly intelligent efforts of the judges of the Supreme Court in the Reference.

---

[82] Débat sur le discours d'ouverture, le chef de l'Opposition officielle, M. Jean Charest; débats de l'Assemblée nationale (4 March 1999).

[83] "L'avis de la Cour suprême sur la sécession du Québec, rendu il y a tout juste un an aujourd'hui, est probablement le plus grand arrêt que notre Cour aura rendu en 124 ans d'existence, qui pourrait devenir un classique du droit constitutionnel contemporain." Patrice Garant, Professor of constitutional law, Université Laval, writing in *Le Devoir* on the anniversary of the Reference judgment (20 August 1999).